To All the Saints
Paul's Letter to the Church at Philippi

Second Edition

Rebecca Minelga

Copyright © 2023 by Rebecca Minelga
All rights reserved. This book or any portion thereof may not be reproduced or used in any manner whatsoever without the express written permission of the publisher except for the use of brief quotations in a book review or scholarly journal.
First Printing: 2016
ISBN 978-0-9982974-2-2

Minelga Press
4407 Tom Marks Rd
Snohomish, WA 98290
www.rminelga.wordpress.com

Scripture quotations taken from the (NASB®) New American Standard Bible®, Copyright © 1960, 1971, 1977, 1995 by The Lockman Foundation. Used by permission. All rights reserved.
www.lockman.org

For Eric, who has always believed in me.

I am also forever indebted to the kindness and support of Jan Kochendorfer and Barbara Walls, and the expertise of Pastor Ben Andrus and Sondra Hirsch. Thank you.

Table of Contents

Foreword to the Second Edition	1
Introduction	3
Reference Notes	8
Paul's Early Ministry	11
Council at Jerusalem	20
Arguments and Appointments	28
Arrival in Philippi	41
Trouble in Philippi	48
Departing Philippi	58
Introducing Philippians	68
A Moment to Reflect	83
Grace to You and Peace	90
The Greater Progress of the Gospel	103
To Live is Christ and to Die is Gain	113
Make My Joy Complete	125
Work Out Your Salvation	137
Hold Men Like Him in High Regard	155
The Righteousness Which Comes from God	167
Join in Following My Example	179
In the Lord	189
The Grace of the Lord Jesus Christ Be with You	209
A Woven Tapestry	223
The Journey's End	231
Bibliography	235

Foreword to the Second Edition

Taking on a second edition is an endeavor fraught with difficulty. While some things *must* change, many others *may*, and it is here that I find myself a bit in the weeds. Since the original publication in 2016, I have written three more books, matured in my faith, and grown in my ministry. In all honesty, I could as easily rewrite this book from scratch as revise it. Nevertheless, I must have faith that what God has begun, He will be faithful to complete. I am a different person today than I was seven years ago, but newer books can attest to that fact, while this one can remain in the place it was originally written, hopefully to continue the good work it began then.

Thus, I have limited my revisions to two main areas. First, I have removed the entirety of the Biblical text of Philippians. Though meant as an aid to those who might not wish to interrupt their reading by opening their Bible, nevertheless, I am compelled to do so, and I am happy to do so, because I do believe that a vibrant life must always orient itself back towards the very Word of God. Therefore, I beseech you, dear Reader, not to breeze past the opportunity to read the very text God breathed through the pen of Paul, but to pause at every invitation and return, again, to your Bible.

Second, I have very gently edited some sentences for technical clarity. I've often believed Paul's letters would be more accessible were he (or his translators) to employ a good, old Oxford comma, but the experience of writing my last few books has taught me a great deal about the value of brevity. Thus, in some instances I have reduced long, complex sentences into a shorter, more comprehensible style. The same goes for some lengthy paragraphs.

Introduction

I'm not sure exactly when I fell in love with Paul's letter to the Church of Philippi, but when the women's group at our church approached me about helping to teach a Bible study, it seemed a natural fit. Of course, God moves; so when I mentioned my passion for Philippians, my co-leader quickly flipped open her Bible and commented, "Oh, look! And it has four chapters!" Given that we had five weeks to fill at the end of a quarter, it seemed providential.

It is a vast undertaking to teach a Bible study, and the words of James have echoed through my mind on more than one occasion: "Let not many of you become teachers, my brethren, knowing that as such we will incur a stricter judgment" (James 3:1). This has long been both the call and challenge of my life: to rise up and meet the heightened expectations of those who might be honored to be called *teacher*, while still maintaining the humility and respect necessary to recognize one's own short-comings and the inherent sinful nature of our human hearts. My pride hath gone before my fall often enough to make me wary of pursuing avenues which might tempt me to self-adoration.

Fortunately, God met me throughout, reminding me at every turn that this was about sharing His heart with the women of our group. When I began to believe I might have all the answers, He was quick to rebuke me through the gentle corrections and spirit of my co-leader. When I became too academic, He used the voices of our participants to remind me that we study the Word in order to become wise, not simply knowledgeable. When I had planned a complex lesson on the spiritual nature of a certain topic, He provided a prophet among us who spoke of her own wretched journey to finding joy in the midst of great and desperate pain.

With so many commentaries on Philippians already in existence, the problem often became more an issue of pruning than discovery. Among dozens of pages of notes available on each and every verse, it became critical to listen to the still, small voice of God, pressing us this way or that, seeking to bring His presence to our very specific group of women. Like Elijah on the mountain, the voice of the Lord was not in the wind, nor in the earthquake, nor in the fire, but "after the fire a sound of a gentle blowing" (1 Kings 19:12b). In light of that fact, we chose to focus on some areas, while leaving others to be taken very much at face value. It would be impossible to fully encompass the breadth of Paul's teaching to the Church of Philippi in five months, never mind five short weeks. As I sought to convert this study to book format, again, I was required to carefully and prayerfully lift up each verse and phrase, knowing that the audience here would be much vaster, with infinitely more needs to be met.

However, I leaned on the promise of God that we need only "ask, and it will be given to you; seek, and you will find; knock, and it will be opened to you. For everyone who asks receives, and he who seeks finds, and to him who knocks it will be opened" (Matthew 7:7-8). God already knows those whom He has divinely appointed to join me on this journey. He has already sought out and, by faith, placed these very words directly into the hands of the one who is seeking Him, today.

I had several purposes in mind in writing this book, which I hope you will see reflected throughout. The first is the importance of understanding the social, cultural, economic, political, and historical contexts of Biblical study. Words that we might gloss over without noting suddenly shimmer into iridescent brilliance as we better understand their significance. Paul wrote from a time of immense upheaval, both politically and religiously, as the new Christian religion sought to take hold past the death of its figurehead.

Understanding the many ways in which Paul wrote from within his own paradigm, as well as the changing paradigm of belief at the time, will more fully inform our own study of his writings.

Second, I believe that anyone can study the Bible. We have seen a revolution of technology in the last generation that will be more lasting and impactful than that of Gutenberg's press. Less than a decade ago, while attending Bible college, I was required to spend thousands of dollars on reference books in order to study the Word of God. Ten short years later, such tomes as *Strong's Exhaustive Concordance*, *Easton's Bible Dictionary*, the *International Standard Bible Encyclopedia*, and so many more are widely available on the internet. Study websites and open-source data allow us to exhaustively study the Bible in a personal and intimate way never before seen. No longer is Biblical study limited to those who can afford the reference material, those well-versed in Latin, Greek, Aramaic, or Hebrew, those with access to higher education and exegetical theory. Hundreds of commentaries, sermons, sermon notes, discussions, and theses are immediately available with only a few keystrokes. I have heavily relied on these sources in writing this book in an effort to model how easy it is for you (yes, you) to do the same. My hope is that your study will not end with the closing pages of this book, but will continue far beyond, utilizing many of the same tools I, myself, have used.

Of course, we must be wise and discerning, as well, remembering that no commentary, no sermon, no theological summation should be considered without first testing it against the divinely inspired, God-breathed Word. Perhaps we are in as much danger today as the Church of Galatia once was, of being led astray by new and dangerous doctrines, of believing in cultural Christianity or a "cult-of-self" built around a single, fallible person, rather than the infallible God. It is only by setting these doctrines against the Bible that we might see truth. I hope then, too, that you will do the same here. My prayer is that I have adequately and authentically portrayed the Word through my understanding, through discernment and the Holy Spirit, through prayerful consideration and with cautiousness that I neither add nor subtract from His purposes. Yet I encourage you, even exhort you, to carefully consider all that you read here against the Word. It is only after doing so that anyone ought to accept any teaching on any Biblical topic.

From His heart to yours, then, dear friend, please be blessed as we explore Paul's Epistle to the Philippians together.

Reference Notes

Due to my desire to model the ease with which one might study the Bible while using online references, I have relied heavily on a number of well-respected Bible websites. First among these has been Blue Letter Bible (www.blueletterbible.org), which has the advantage of an integrated interlinear word study feature that includes both Strong's Concordance and Larry Pierce's *Outline of Biblical Usage*, of which Blue Letter Bible explains,

> We used the Strong's system with the actual Greek and Hebrew to implement the numbers. By doing this we obtained about 15000 corrections in the Strong's concordance by using the work of Larry Pierce, the author of the Online Bible (OLB – a Bible program for PC and Mac).
>
> Larry Pierce combined what Dr. Strong cited with Smith's Bible Dictionary and Dr. Thayer cited in his abridged Thayer's 1889 Greek-

English Lexicon. It is keyed to Kittel's "Theological Dictionary of the New Testament." This resulted in the Greek Definitions module for the OLB. Online Bible also altered Thayer's definitions concerning the Holy Spirit and the divinity of Christ since Thayer was a Unitarian. Larry and the developers of OLB did the same with the Old Testament in that they combined Dr. Strong's citings with Brown, Driver, and Briggs' work on the Gesenius Lexicon; this is keyed to the "Theological Word Book of the Old Testament." (Help :: Help Tutorials n.d.)

You will note throughout this book that all word usage studies have been tagged with their Strong's Concordance numbers; however, they have been accessed using Larry Pierce's system on Blue Letter Bible, which combines multiple sources for the truest rendering of word meanings. Due to the complex nature of appropriately citing this type of reference, all such citations read, *BLB 2016, Strong's G####*. By this you will know that it was accessed using the system described above and does not, in fact, match the traditional *Strong's Exhaustive Concordance* citations.

Additionally, unless marked otherwise, all Bible citations throughout come from the New American Standard Bible (NASB). Due to the many abbreviations commonly accepted for each individual book, as well as the easy confusion between Philippians (which will embody the majority of our study) and Philemon in terms of these abbreviations, I have chosen to fully write out each reference.

Paul's Early Ministry

The story of Philippians begins with Paul. Yet, it does not begin with the venerated Paul of the Pauline Letters which make up nearly half of our New Testament. Wise and temperate, truly a father of the early church, the Paul we see through the lens of his letters to his beloved brethren is very different than the Paul to whom we are first introduced. No, instead it begins with a much younger Paul, stretching backwards across the years to all those pieces of him that needed refining and tempering, to a fateful day on a dirt road near Damascus, to a friendship struck from the ashes of a life left behind. To understand Paul is to understand his writings more richly.

Moreover, a thorough understanding of the historical, cultural, and socio-political aspects of the first century is absolutely required to fully encompass the richness of Paul's teachings. Paul's visit to Philippi hardly took place within a vacuum, either spiritually or contextually, nor did he write his letter to them from a vaunted position of absolute neutrality or omniscience. He often wrote in response to current events, challenges to the church from both within and without, and the persecution that the early church faced in its infancy. Conflict with Rome, the history of the Law, dissension between Jewish and Greek Christians, and the prevailing philosophies of life itself, all garnered Paul's attention and, thus, warrant ours as well if we are seeking to fully comprehend the subtle nuances of his teachings.

Paul's Conversion

Paul's first foray into sustained, long-term missions came during his first missionary journey, which is chronicled in Acts 13-14. Prior even to that was his own, rather dramatic conversion in Acts 9, which set the stage for both Paul's missionary heart and enacted the very circumstances that would later lead to both his first and second missionary journeys. God's divine appointments are never by accident, and Saul's appointment with Christ on the road to Damascus was no exception. The very voice of Jesus thundered from the heavens, calling Paul to account, demanding a response: "Saul, Saul, why are you persecuting me?" (Acts 9:4)

Nor was his divine appointment with Ananias an accident. In his commentary on Acts 9, David Guzik says of this previously unknown man:

> Why Ananias? Was he a prominent Christian? We have no reason to believe so. Did God need to use a human agent at all in this work? Not really. God used Ananias because God loves to use people, and Ananias was a willing servant.
>
> Ananias was an ordinary man – not an apostle, a prophet, a pastor, an evangelist, an elder, or a deacon. Yet God used him especially because he was an ordinary man. If an apostle or a prominent person had ministered to Paul, people might say Paul received his gospel from a man instead of Jesus. In the same way, God needs to use the ordinary man – there is a special work for them to do. (Guzik 2001a)

Nor, ultimately, was Paul's divine appointment with Barnabas an accident.

> When he came to Jerusalem, he was trying to associate with the disciples; but they were all afraid of him, not believing that he was a disciple. But Barnabas took hold of him and brought him to the apostles and described to them how he had seen the Lord on the road, and that He had talked to him, and how at Damascus he had spoken out boldly in the name of Jesus. (Acts 9:26-27)

Barnabas would go on to become one of Paul's closest friends, a true brother in Christ, ministering beside him both abroad and at home. No, this appointment was most certainly not accidental, for it was to set the stage for far greater things to come, both astounding workings of the Holy Spirit as well as the guiding hand of God as He worked all things for His glory, even the minor and petty disputes of the greatest men of the early church.

It is arguable that Paul never had a chance meeting in his entire ministry. From the day of his conversion until the day of his death, we see nothing but an on-going record of Paul's desire to preach the word of God and the salvation of Jesus Christ with boldness and passion, but also with logic and common sense. In the story of the Philippian Church alone, we see any number of chance meetings, faithfully fulfilled to the salvation of many: Lydia, the possessed servant girl, and the Jailer. Earlier still, Paul's introduction to Timothy could be considered to be purely by chance; however, we know better. Timothy would go on to become one of the foremost leaders of the second generation after Christ's death, beloved of Paul as a son, and an exceptional missionary in his own right.

God's faithfulness has not abated even today. Divine appointments from the Creator come every day. Some are small and risk being lost in the hectic busyness of everyday life: a smile from a stranger, a word of encouragement to someone struggling, a hug for a child, a quick prayer of healing, thanksgiving, or blessing. Some are far larger. Whether large or small, however, God uses people, people like you and I, to fulfill His purposes, if only we are willing.

Why do I spend so much time to say this? Because you, beloved, have just begun a divine appointment. When you choose to dig deeper into the Word of God, when you meet Him in His holy places, when you commit yourself to prayer and spiritual teaching, you open the door for a divine appointment with the Heavenly Father, Himself. And He, in turn, will open the door to other divine appointments, bringing people into your life who need a word or who have one for you. Whatever moved within you to choose this book off a shelf, to pick it from a line-up of digital covers, it is the Holy Spirit moving in you, and in faith, I believe that God will bring a Word of Truth to you through this reading.

As I have already said, God knows who will be joining me on this journey. God already knows YOU. Let there be no mistake: God has desired for you a divine appointment with His Word, and he will be faithful to fulfill that promise. In Isaiah, God speaks through the prophet, saying, "so will My word be which goes forth from My mouth; it will not return to Me empty, without accomplishing what I desire, and without succeeding in the matter for which

I sent it" (Isaiah 55:11). In the vernacular of the church today, God's word will not return void, and His work in you will not return void, either. As it did in Paul, it will work in you and through you, for the glory of God, if only you will let it.

Paul's First Missionary Journey

After a period of some time, certainly more than a year (Acts 11:26 says that Paul and Barnabas ministered together at Antioch for at least that long), Paul and Barnabas received a calling from God to go forth, chronicled in Acts 13:2. This, then, is the moment at which God calls them out, paired, as in Mark 6:7 and Luke 10:1, to begin the work of spreading the Gospel to all the world. They were not the first, certainly, but they likely were the first to venture beyond the city of Antioch and continue northwards into the area that is now modern-day Turkey. In fact, in undertaking this journey, it is arguable that they may have been responsible for doubling the distance that the Word had traveled since the death and resurrection of Christ or the events of the Day of Pentecost described in Acts 2.

Prior to Paul and Barnabas' journey, the Gospel was somewhat well-spread from Jerusalem to the fledgling church at Antioch by such individuals as Peter, John, Stephen (the first martyr, at whose death Saul, himself, stood by), and Philip. However, the reach beyond Antioch to the north, and

Jerusalem to the south, would have been virtually nonexistent.

As a reformed Jew, himself, one who had begun as one of the worst persecutors of the early church and was now quickly being regarded as one of its greatest spokesmen, it is no wonder that Paul sought first to preach the Good News to other Jews. Of course, as we see in Acts 13-14, while many were receptive, many more virulently disagreed with Paul's teaching. In Acts 13, we see Paul's response:

> But when the Jews saw the crowds, they were filled with jealousy and began contradicting the things spoken by Paul, and were blaspheming. Paul and Barnabas spoke out boldly, and said, "It was necessary that the word of God be spoken to you first; since you repudiate it and judge yourselves unworthy of eternal life, behold, we are turning to the Gentiles." (Acts 13:45-46)

Strong words against those who ought to have been, both politically and religiously, their closest brethren. Only a few verses later, "they shook off the dust of their feet in protest against them" (Acts 13:51a) and departed.

Even as he made a physical journey to spread the Gospel Message, Paul was undergoing a spiritual journey as well, one that would later shape the heart and soul of his ministry. A Jew among Jews, there is no doubt Paul believed that the Jewish people were the first sons and daughters of the Most High. He often referred to the promises of God to Abraham and Moses and referred to the people of Israel as the chosen of God. However, it is at this moment, on the steps of a synagogue in Pisidian Antioch (not the same Antioch from whence they had set out), that the core of Paul's ministry underwent a drastic shift in focus.

While Paul continued to preach in synagogues and to his Jewish brethren, Guzik notes, "Paul shows wisdom in not spending all his time trying to persuade hardened hearts" (Guzik 2001b). He never ceased to desire for the redemption of all Israel (see Romans 10:1), but the heart of his ministry now began to shift towards those with more open hearts, and, especially, the Gentiles.

It is critical to understand the journey that Paul's ministry took in its early years to fully understand the impact that he would later have. It was amidst these formative experiences during his first time traveling as an itinerant preacher in Jesus' Name, that he might have begun to better understand Jesus' words during the Sermon on the Mount.

> Blessed are those who have been persecuted for the sake of righteousness, for theirs is the kingdom of heaven. Blessed are you when people insult you and persecute you, and falsely say all kinds of evil against you because of Me. Rejoice and be glad, for your reward in heaven is great; for in

the same way they persecuted the prophets who were before you. (Matthew 5:10-12)

So incredibly impactful were both Jesus' teaching and his own experiences that Paul later wrote, in direct response to the kind of reception he received from his Jewish brethren, "I count all things to be loss in view of the surpassing knowledge of knowing Christ Jesus my Lord, for whom I have suffered the loss of all things, and count them but rubbish so that I may gain Christ" (Philippians 3:8).

It is thus that we begin to see the importance of fully understanding what came before Paul's second missionary journey, the experiences he had which shaped his later ministry, and the developing understanding he was gaining as he began to find the purpose to which God had called him.

The Council at Jerusalem

As Paul and Barnabas returned from this first joint effort, they discovered that their own experiences amongst both the Jews and the Gentiles were being reflected in the larger community of the fledgling Church. Peter, too, had run afoul of a Jewish system that did not encompass the possibility that Gentiles might henceforth, with the death and resurrection of Jesus Christ, be admitted as brothers before the Lord. Throughout the first half of Acts, Peter is often to be found preaching boldly for the inclusion of Gentiles amidst the early believers. This is borne out more than once as God poured out signs and wonders over the newly converted Gentiles.

Peter in Jerusalem

Ten years earlier, while in Caesarea on his own missionary journey, Peter is recorded as speaking the Gospel message in the home of Cornelius. As he concludes, we read:

> While Peter was still speaking these words, the Holy Spirit fell upon all those who were listening to the message. All the circumcised believers who came with Peter were amazed, because the gift of the Holy Spirit had been poured out on the Gentiles also. For they were hearing them speaking with tongues and exalting God. Then Peter answered, "Surely no one can refuse the water for these to be baptized who have received the Holy Spirit just as we did, can he?" (Acts 10:44-47)

Like Paul later would, Peter had discovered that not only was there resistance among his own kinsmen and open hearts among the Gentiles, but that God, Himself, seemed to be pouring out His blessing over the Gentiles who were tender enough to receive His word. In fact, upon recounting the events of his journey in Caesarea to those still at Jerusalem, Peter set the stage for the later Council at Jerusalem, in which both Peter and Paul testified to the work of the Holy Spirit among the Gentiles.

One thing is clear: within the early Church, the role of the Gentile inside the Kingdom of God was not yet fully understood or defined. Paul would prove to be not only a critical component in further understanding God's will for the uncircumcised, he would also become one of their greatest advocates and missionaries.

Upon returning from their northern journey, Paul and Barnabas decided to travel to Jerusalem to help answer the increasingly vexing question of what role Gentiles ought to play in the infant Church. Their decision was hastened by false teachings being spread throughout the region that only those Gentiles who submitted themselves to both circumcision and the Law were acceptable in God's eyes. While Peter's journey to Caesarea nearly a decade earlier had cemented the fact that Gentiles could, indeed, be saved, Paul's journey would be the one to define the necessary extent of their adhesion to Jewish custom and law.

The Council at Jerusalem

While Gentiles continued to swell the ranks of the early church, it is important to note that at this time, probably around 48CE, the majority, if not all, of the leaders within this early Christ-movement were converted Jews. Of course, the Apostles were well known, and many continued to preach the gospel and tell of their experiences living daily with the Messiah. Matthew and John would go on to canonically chronicle these events, and all but two of the Apostles would go on to be martyred for their faith. The two exceptions were

Judas, who committed suicide, and John, who died later in life after receiving the prophetic dreams that he later recorded in the Book of Revelation, the final chapter of the modern Bible. Peter and John would both go on to pen their own New Testament letters. Alongside them, others began to have an impact on the early church, including men such as Paul and Barnabas; then, later, Timothy, Silas, and Titus, and, most especially, James, the brother of Jesus, and writer of the Book of James. It was he who, from his position of authority, heard the testimonies of Peter, Paul, and Barnabas in Jerusalem.

James had his own, troublesome journey to becoming an early leader within the Church. Beth Moore's *Mercy Triumphs* is a beautiful rendition of both the biography of James and the letter which bears his name. Raised with his brother Jesus, he seemed content to ridicule and mock the Savior, until, after Jesus' death and resurrection, he was paid a visit by his risen brother. Like Paul, James' is a dramatic story of redemption at the foot of the resurrected Christ. Of James' ascension within the Church, Moore says this:

> After his saving encounter with the resurrected Christ, James must have resided in Jerusalem and ended up working alongside Peter. In the early years of Christianity, Peter was the unchallenged leader of the budding church in and around Jerusalem. This position shifted to James, however, and Acts 12:17 probably best explains why. (Moore 2011, 25)

The verse referenced informs us that Peter is compelled to leave Jerusalem, probably around 42CE, and, specifically, asks that the brethren relay the news of his dramatic prison escape to James (Acts 12:1-19). In effect, Peter fled Jerusalem to escape Herod and very intentionally left a successor in his place. James spent the ensuing years carefully crafting a faith-driven body of believers within Jerusalem and its surrounding environs and attentively studying both the written Word of God in the Old Testament and the spoken word of the Gospel messages being preached by those who had walked with Jesus, witnessed the performing of His miracles, or received His healing touch themselves.

It is thus that Peter and Paul, along with Barnabas, returned to Jerusalem to stand before James, as well as John, to argue their case. Peter began by speaking passionately of the outpouring that the Holy Spirit imbued within the Gentile believers, making "no distinction between us and them, cleansing their hearts by faith" (Acts 15:9). Then, he continued, challenging, "Now therefore why do you put God to the test by placing upon the neck of the disciples a yoke which neither our fathers nor we have been able to bear?" (Acts 15:10). He finished with this fervent statement: "But we believe that we are saved through the grace of the Lord Jesus, in the same way as they also are" (Acts 15:11).

These were impactful words, a direct challenge to the difficult nature of attaining and maintaining the discipline of the Law, and an ardent plea for the recognition of the fundamental differences in faith that a Gentile would possess. In essence, Peter argued that since no one had yet managed to fully encompass the Law of the Old Testament, Jew or otherwise, and since Christ had abolished it anyway by grace through faith, then what purpose remained for requiring the Gentiles to submit therein?

Then it was Paul and Barnabas' turn to speak. We are told little, simply that they relayed "what signs and wonders God had done through them among the Gentiles" (Acts 15:12). Finally, James, as the premier Jewish Christian leader of the Church, spoke. In a moving oration, he told of the testimony of those who had worked among the Gentiles, bringing the Word of God and seeing the outpouring of the Holy Spirit. He stated, "Therefore it is my judgment that we do not trouble those who are turning to God from among the Gentiles" (Acts 15:19). He goes on to list a few points that might remain contentious between Jewish and Gentile Christians, asking for forbearance and respect from their new brethren as Jewish Christians continued to practice many of the cultural aspects of their initial faith and maintained many of the same rules which had been instituted by God for their protection against idolatry. In a letter, they tell the new Gentile Christians at Antioch, Syria, and Cilicia,

> "For it seemed good to the Holy Spirit and to us to lay upon you no greater burden than the essentials: that you abstain from things sacrificed to idols and from blood and things strangled and from fornication; if you keep yourself free from such things, you will do well" (Acts 15:28-29).

It is unlikely that a matter of this magnitude was, in fact, decided so quickly and amongst so few people as is recorded in Acts. Fortunately, in Galatians, Paul recalls his time in Jerusalem and is able to elaborate a few more details for us. After speaking of "false brethren" who desired to see the Gentiles enslaved to the Law, Paul says:

> But we did not yield in subjection to them for even an hour, so that the truth of the gospel would remain with you. But from those who were of high reputation (what they were makes no difference to me; God shows no partiality)—well, those who were of reputation contributed nothing to me. But on the contrary, seeing that I had been entrusted with the gospel to the uncircumcised, just as Peter had been to the circumcised (for He who effectually worked for Peter in his apostleship to the circumcised effectually worked for me also to the Gentiles), and recognizing the grace that had been given to me, James and Cephas [Peter] and John, who were reputed to be pillars, gave

> to me and Barnabas the right hand of fellowship, so that we might go to the Gentiles and they to the circumcised. They only asked us to remember the poor— the very thing I also was eager to do. (Galatians 2:5-10).

Paul paints a vivid picture of political maneuvering, deft interception and intercession, and a dramatic finale that encompassed not only his ultimate purpose in appealing to the brethren at Jerusalem, but also his acceptance among those vaunted leaders of the early Church. This was a crucial turning point in Paul's public ministry. He was no longer merely an itinerant preacher, but now had been embraced by the leadership in Jerusalem and charged to go forth, preaching the Gospel of Jesus Christ.

Arguments and Appointments

Paul wasted little time, immediately returning to Antioch and commencing the planning for his second missionary journey. Riding the victory of the Council at Jerusalem, one might think that Paul's return and subsequent departure from Antioch might be a laureled victory march; however, wherever there is great revival, the enemy also creates great resistance, and this was true for Paul, as well. Rather than setting forth on his second missionary journey in a blaze of triumph, Paul was instead forced to confront deeply unsettling personal conflict, the likes of which nearly fractured the burgeoning church.

Paul and Barnabas

As Paul and Barnabas began to plan their journey to visit the churches they'd planted during their first missionary journey, we discover their challenge.

> After some days Paul said to Barnabas, "Let us return and visit the brethren in every city in which we proclaimed the word of the Lord, and see how they are." Barnabas wanted to take John, called Mark, along with them also. But Paul kept insisting that they should not take him along who had deserted them in Pamphylia and had not gone with them to the work. And there occurred such a sharp disagreement that they separated from one another… (Acts 15:36-39a)

The impact of this disagreement rocked the early church, and it was so divisive in nature that the very words used to describe this conflict are steeped in nuanced and subtle meaning.

One word, in particular, becomes important to fully understand this text: the Greek word that is used to explain their "sharp disagreement," *paroxysmos* (BLB 2016, Strong's G3948). This is the same root word for our own English word *paroxysm* and is considered synonymous with such other words as *spasm, attack, fit, burst, outburst, eruption,* or *explosion*. Literally translated, their disagreement was not only "sharp" in nature, it was literally an explosion between them; an explosion that threatened to take the rest of the newly-founded Christian Church with them. The visual we are left with is of two men, both stalwart in their views, crossing sharpened swords, neither willing to back down.

What was it, then, that was so inciting about this incident that the two split, never, apparently, to be fully reconciled? Bosom friends since Barnabas had been the first to welcome Paul to the Christian fold seven years earlier, traveling companions across the Eastern Mediterranean and Turkey, fellow workers in Christ who planted numerous churches and defended the freedom of the Gentiles from the Law together in Jerusalem, and this one seemingly small issue tore them apart. It is hard to imagine that anything might provide an acceptable catalyst for this situation; nevertheless, one apparently existed.

The two differed over who might accompany them on their second journey together. Barnabas wanted John Mark, his nephew, to be permitted to join them. Paul, remembering John Mark's behavior on their previous journey, declined. "Now Paul and his companions put out to sea from Paphos and came to Perga in Pamphylia; but John left them and returned to Jerusalem" (Acts 13:13). Interestingly, the Holman Christian Standard Bible (HCSB) translates "return" as "went back," and Young's Literal Translation (YLT) translates it as "turn back," which may give us a better understanding of why his actions were so unacceptable to Paul. If, in the face of previous hardship, John Mark's faith had waivered to the extent that he turned back, what would he do on this journey? Meanwhile,

Barnabas, already well known to be gentle and tender-hearted (see Acts 4:36 and Acts 9:26-27), was willing to give John Mark a second chance.

Luke, in writing Acts, does not seem to give us an indication of who was, in fact, in the right. As with most disagreements of this nature, it is likely that each was somewhat culpable for the situation. Some commentators suggest that family ties made Barnabas more susceptible to the kind of nepotism described. Others suggest that his gentle heart would have been better heeded by Paul, who had already once benefited from it, himself (see Acts 9:26-27). In any case, the two were resolutely divided, and as Acts picks up the thread of Paul's continuing ministry, the name of Barnabas is all but obliterated from the remainder of the New Testament.

Thus, we see, "Barnabas took Mark with him and sailed away to Cyprus. But Paul chose Silas and left, being committed by the brethren to the grace of the Lord" (Acts 14:39b-40). It would be Barnabas who would return to the church plants that he and Paul had first tended together. Paul, accompanied by Silas, and later Timothy, set off on a new journey to bring the Gospel Message to the European Continent.

It is, however, encouraging to note that, while a reconciliation between the two friends is not recorded, Paul obviously learned from the experience. In Ephesians, he counsels,

> Do not grieve the Holy Spirit of God, by whom you were sealed for the day of redemption. Let all bitterness and wrath and anger and clamor and slander be put away from you, along with all malice. Be kind to one another, tender-hearted, forgiving each other, just as God in Christ also has forgiven you. (Ephesians 4:30-32)

We will see this same advice from Paul to two members of the Church at Philippi in just a little while.

Further, in 2 Timothy, Paul directly references the restoration of his relationship with John Mark, where, after listing all those fellow workers who have deserted him, he says, "Only Luke is with me. Pick up Mark and bring him with you, for he is useful to me for service" (2 Timothy 4:11). It is interesting to note that, while absolute authorship is impossible to establish, it is generally agreed upon that it is this same Mark, cousin of Barnabas, deserter of Paul, who wrote the Gospel of Mark, most likely around the same time that Paul was writing to the Philippians. There is certainly no doubt that John Mark had his own divine appointments to meet, and that he and Paul must have crossed paths again, at some point, and mended their relationship.

One of the things that makes Paul so fascinating is the glimpse we receive into his innate humanity. Far from being an unshakable pillar of faith, the Bible records for us a number of instances where he genuinely struggled to remain faithful to the call he had received. He, like us, needed time, knowledge, and wisdom to mature into the Apostle that we remember him to be. Experiencing his journey should be encouraging to any believer who has ever struggled with similar issues; Paul speaks of his arrogance and pride, his anger, and the "thorn" in his side, an unnamed condition that plagued his entire life. We read of moments like this one, where his temper overcame even the needs of the church, and he failed to walk in the Spirit of God.

As we close out our penultimate verses of Acts and press forward, it is important to note that Acts records for us a young man full of fiery passion and the Holy Spirit. Paul's later Epistles show us a mature church leader who, with the benefit of a full life lived in the shadow of the Most High, has learned wisdom at the feet of the Father. Let us remember, then, that many of us are as Paul was in Acts, young and fiery, headstrong, impatient, full of the Spirit, and impassioned. As we study the wisdom of his later years, let us remember, too, that it is collected over a lifetime of God's perfect provision. Like Paul, let us strive ever forward, pressing onwards towards the goal, in Christ's name.

Silas and Timothy

With the stage now set, we turn, finally, to Luke's recording of Paul's second journey. As Acts 15 closes, we are left with these words: "But Paul chose Silas and left, being committed by the brethren to the grace of the Lord. And he was traveling through Syria and Cilicia, strengthening the churches" (Acts 15:40-41). Barnabas and John Mark have since departed to Cyprus, intent on visiting those churches first planted by Paul and Barnabas, and into the breach of Barnabas' perceived betrayal steps Silas (also known as Silvanus in the New Testament). With his dearest friend now rent from him, Paul was about to embark on a new missionary journey with a new companion, one he most certainly knew; however, there was still uncertainty.

Paul was a man who was shaped by his experiences, much as we all are. I can't help but wonder what might have been running through his mind as he again departed Antioch, Silas by his side. Did he worry that a similar disruption might occur between them? Did his heart continue to yearn for Barnabas and remember fondly their first journey together? Was he hesitant to trust this new traveling companion?

I think it likely he also would have wondered what purposes God was seeking to fulfill. As what was arguably his deepest friendship seemed to crumble around him, I wonder if he began his journey in anguish, crying out to God in supplication, asking, as we so often do, *God, what did I do wrong? How could You have let this happen? What are You doing here?* Or perhaps he was still angry, demanding an account of God's actions. *God, why have you done this to me? Were we not faithful? Are You, then, unfaithful?* Or perhaps he set out weighted down by the burden of his own sins, the realization already crashing over him that his quick temper was much to blame for the ensuing conflict, his inherent sinfulness deeming him fully unworthy of the calling placed upon him. Certainly, this is a reaction I can relate to. *How can I serve You, God, when I can't even keep my temper in check, when I alienate even those who love me best through my own sinfulness and unworthiness?*

Perhaps God, hearing the cries of Paul's heart, had compassion upon him.

In time, Silas would grow to become a friend Paul trusted, remaining with him for the duration of his second missionary journey and often referred to throughout his epistles. God also provided to Paul a new companion, Timothy, a young man of Lystra.

Timothy would become one of Paul's closest friends, eclipsing all others, Silas and Barnabas included. He was a man often referred to as being "like a son" to the apostle, one trusted and entrusted with the teaching of the Gospel message in his absence. Later, Paul would say of Timothy, "For I have no one else of kindred spirit…but you know of his proven worth" (Philippians 2:20, 22), and "who is my beloved and faithful child in the Lord" (1 Corinthians 4:17). It is clear, then, that this meeting would continue to grow and blossom into as deep a relationship as any Paul would ever have.

In fact, it is hard to believe that Paul's introduction to Timothy, a young man of both Jewish and Greek descent, at the outset of what would become a missionary journey primarily to the Gentiles of Europe, was by happenstance only. Indeed, with Paul's history of divine appointments, I think it is safe to argue that God, once again moving mightily, not only heard the outcry of Paul's heart in the wake of Barnabas' defection but sought to amply and abundantly bless Paul on his journey with not only one, but two boon companions, to ease his way.

It is either a prodigious compliment to the heart of Barnabas that it took two men to replace him, or a tremendous testimony to the abundant life of Christ Jesus that Paul's loss was replaced doubly replaced. As in the Old Testament, "The Lord restored the fortunes of Job when he prayed for his friends, and the Lord increased all that Job had twofold" (Job 42:10). I do not think we need to make too big a leap to believe that Paul, perhaps fully convicted by the Holy Spirit, might have repented of his behavior towards Barnabas and gone on to authentically pray not only for his

Brother in Christ, but also for the work he was doing among the churches that Paul so loved. And God, seeing both the tenderness of Paul's heart and the genuine sincerity of spirit with which that prayer was offered, may have seen fit to respond with the kind of abundant blessing that Paul would later remember as the hallmark of God's provision.

In any case, it was here, right at the start of their journey, that Timothy joined Paul and Silas. However, before continuing any further, it is important to note one small detail of their introduction that could easily be glossed over, or worse, misinterpreted entirely. In describing their initial meeting, Luke says,

> Paul came also to Derbe and to Lystra. And a disciple was there, named Timothy, the son of a Jewish woman who was a believer, but his father was a Greek, and he was well spoken of by the brethren who were in Lystra and Iconium. Paul wanted this man to go with him; and he took him and circumcised him because of the Jews who were in those parts, for they all knew that his father was a Greek. (Acts 16:1-3)

Having just completed their journey to Jerusalem to secure the rights of the Gentile not to be circumcised, why, then, does Paul insist on this act before Timothy can accompany them? The answer, it seems, lies not in the spiritual, but in the practical. In his *Exposition of the Entire Bible*, John Gill writes that Paul,

> took and circumcised him [Timothy]; which may seem strange, when there had been so lately a controversy in the church at Antioch about circumcision, from whence the apostle was just come; and when this matter had been debated and determined by the apostles and elders at Jerusalem, where he was present, and he was now carrying about their decrees: but it is to be observed, that the apostle used circumcision not as a duty of the law, as what that required, and in obedience to it, which he knew was abrogated; much less as necessary to salvation, which the Judaizing preachers urged; but as an indifferent thing, and in order to gain a point, and secure some valuable end, as follows
>
> because[*sic*] of the Jews which were in those quarters; not the believing ones, for he brought along with him the decrees of the apostles and elders to satisfy them, that circumcision was not necessary; but the unbelieving ones, who he knew would not suffer an uncircumcised person to teach in their synagogues, nor would they hear him out of them; wherefore having a mind to take Timothy with him to be assisting to him in the preaching of the Gospel, in point of prudence he thought it proper to circumcise him, that he might be received by them, and be the more acceptable to them; who would otherwise have taken such an offence at him... (Gill 1999)

Thus, it is explained that Timothy, being half-Jewish on his mother's side, but never having been circumcised because it was a maternal connection, was both Jewish by birth and upbringing, but, nevertheless, had failed to receive the circumcision of his faith. He was, therefore, technically an apostate Jew. Paul, rightfully concerned that this would not only invalidate Timothy's testimony but would also severely discredit his own, insisted that Timothy undergo the procedure. It was not necessary as a sign of his own faith, which the Council at Jerusalem had resoundingly negated, but as a matter of procedure to increase his credibility among the unbelieving Jews.

As with James, Beth Moore has written a striking Bible study on the First and Second Letters to the Thessalonians. In it, she chronicles this same period of time (since Paul's visit to Thessalonica is a part of the same journey as the one to Philippi). As she sets this same backstory, Moore makes two critical observations. The first is, "The next person we meet could become one of the dearest people in our lives" (Moore 2014, 13). Unbeknownst to Paul, in the aftermath of his explosive conflict with Barnabas, he met a young man who would change not only his life, but the lives of the believers of the early church for the glory of God. Next, Moore says, "A journey gone awry could lead to the exact frame of mind God is looking to use"

(Moore 2014, 13). Perhaps these two statements might read better if reversed: *A journey gone awry could lead to the exact frame of mind God is looking to use, and the next person we meet could become one of the dearest people in our lives.* Certainly, this was true of Paul, where the former so informed the latter that a new family model was born, one that the church has since embraced: parents need not be of blood and bone to love and honor children, and children need not be born of parents to learn the wisdom of God at their knee.

If that is not a divine appointment, I don't know what is.

Arrival In Philippi

The cast now set; the journey thus began. Luke tells us that after leaving Lystra, the three companions – Paul, Silas, and Timothy – set out, passing first through Phrygia and Galatia, "having been forbidden by the Holy Spirit to speak the word in Asia" (Acts 16:6). They turn west, making several stops before being led by the Spirit to Macedonia. Crossing the sea from the port city of Troas, they proceed to Samothrace, Neapolis, and, finally, Philippi.

The Via Egnatia

It could be argued that this one journey rewrote the entirety of Western Civilization. Had Paul continued into Asia, perhaps the societies and religions of the Far East might have become the heart of Christian civilization and culture. Instead, Paul, Silas, and Timothy arrived in Neapolis, where they were joined by Luke, the author of Acts, but who is probably better known for having authored the Gospel of Luke.

Reaching Neapolis, we see where this all-important pivot point hinged: the Via Egnatia. It would be hard to overstate the importance of the Via Egnatia to the early dissemination of the Gospel throughout Europe, or, indeed, the divine providence by which Paul and his companions were led to travel by it. No mean dirt road, the Via Egnatia was one of the foremost highways of the Roman kingdom, stretching nearly 700 miles from Byzantium to the Adriatic Sea. Not only lengthy, the Via Egnatia had its origins as a military route, meant to move vast quantities of men, beasts, and weapons to the far-flung fronts of the Roman Empire. As such, it, like other Roman Highways of the day, was nearly twenty feet wide, either paved or heavily sanded to prevent mire and mud and was both well-maintained and well-traveled.

To the Romans, the Via Egnatia was, in essence, a continuation of the all-important Via Appia, the main highway between Rome, itself, and the western shores of the Adriatic. Traveling well-charted sea routes, one could easily journey from Rome to Byzantium along these two highways. And many did: everyone from merchants to pilgrims, soldiers to diplomatic envoys, and more, relied heavily upon the technologically advanced Roman highway system to travel.

Long after Paul and his companions returned from their missionary journey, the Gospel would have continued to spread along this route until it reached the very heart of the Roman Empire, and thence, outwards again into all Roman-controlled provinces.

Lydia, The First European Convert

We are told little about the stop-over in Neapolis. For whatever reason, probably at the prompting of the Holy Spirit, our travelers did not see fit to pause there for very long, instead continuing westward along the Via Egnatia towards Philippi, which is reported as "a leading city in the district of Macedonia, a Roman colony" (Acts 16:12). This description, then, gives us a critical clue as to the nature of God's mission, both in Philippi and, in a larger sense, for their journey: already divinely appointed to travel the Via Egnatia, here is further proof that the Spirit of God had a plan for the conversion of all of Europe. No waypoint or minor port town for the initial dissemination of the Gospel to the European continent, but one of the greatest cities of the region, of strategic political and commercial importance, and the perfect setting from which Paul would launch what is arguably his greatest missionary journey.

Upon arriving in Philippi, Paul's feet hit the ground running.

> And on the Sabbath day we went outside the gate to a riverside, where we were supposing that there would be a place of prayer; and we sat down and began speaking to the women who had assembled.
>
> A woman named Lydia, from the city of Thyatira, a seller of purple fabrics, a worshiper of God, was listening; and the Lord opened her heart to respond to the things spoken by Paul. And when she and her household had been baptized, she urged us, saying, "If you have judged me to be faithful to the Lord, come into my house and stay." And she prevailed upon us. (Acts 16:13-15)

Paul began, as he always did, by speaking first to those of the Jewish faith. Lacking a significant population of male Jews, there was no synagogue in Philippi. As such, Paul sought out the small congregation. F.F. Bruce explains,

> At Philippi, then, they spent several days. When Paul visited a new city, it was his practice, as we have seen, to attend the local Jewish synagogue on the first Sabbath after his arrival and seek an opportunity to make his message known there. At Philippi, however, there does not appear to have been a regular synagogue. That can only mean there were very few resident Jews; had there been ten Jewish men, they would have sufficed to constitute a synagogue. No number of women could compensate for the absence of even one man necessary to make up the quorum of ten. (Bruce 1988, 310)

Bruce's commentary is interesting in that it seems to reflect the very belief of the text he is expositing; that is, the limited value of women in both the Roman and Jewish patriarchal social structures. It is uniquely poignant, then, that God chose a woman for the first European convert. And neither did he choose a wife or a mother (though Lydia may have been both), but a businesswoman: one of powerful social and economic standing. I am reminded of the renowned woman of Proverbs 31, who runs her household and manages the family's affairs with an iron will and a heart of faith.

What, then, can we glean from this narrative? While man may not always value every person in a society, God always sees them. Man or woman, slave or free, Jew or Gentile, God's heart has a place for each and every one of them, and it is no accident that Paul's divine appointment with Lydia might then serve to subvert the traditional social understanding of the day. As Jesus sat to dine with tax collectors and sinners, so, too, did Paul sit beside those whose hearts were open to the Word, no matter their class.

Lydia was a woman of means, and her inclusion in the story of Philippi reminds us of a number of key roles in the dissemination of the Gospel. First, a woman influences her household. As the primary caregivers, women are instrumental in raising their children in faith. Whether a mother, an aunt, a grandmother, or a family friend, children tend to be surrounded first and most by the women in their lives; and the impact this can have on their developing understanding of faith cannot be overstated. Next, Lydia's unique position as a businesswoman in Philippi opened an additional sphere of influence, though one more traditionally attributed to men. She would have been able to use her business contacts – *networking*, as we call it today – to continue spreading the Gospel. The nature of her business, one that involved the importation of luxury goods, would have further broadened her opportunities. Her impact would continue to grow well outside of the confines of Philippi through ongoing transactions; and her audience on both ends, both in receiving the goods from middle class merchants and in selling them to high-ranking Roman officials (the only ones permitted to wear the royal purple), would ensure that those who heard the Gospel would be admirably placed to spread it still farther.

In Lydia, then, we see both the private and public facets of evangelism, both the traditionally masculine and traditionally feminine. Moreover, to see both fully encompassed in a single person reminds us that we each have a similar opportunity and responsibility: to live out Christ's message of love both internally and externally, at home and in our communities, locally and globally. Indeed, it was no mistake that God chose Lydia to be the first European convert.

Trouble in Philippi

With such an auspicious beginning, I can't help but imagine Paul's burgeoning sense of triumph, the belief that, with such an inspiring start, anything might be possible. I wonder, again, if he might have even found himself a bit prideful. Certainly, God likes to take the opportunity to remind us of His sovereignty, especially when we become a bit too self-reliant and self-aggrandizing. Perhaps Paul's "thorn" was not merely limited to the physical but extended so far as to a regular and thorough reliance on God through the many trials he faced. In any case, it doesn't take long for Paul to once again run afoul of local discrimination.

The Possessed Slave Girl

While it is unclear how long Paul and his companions stayed in Philippi, we are given to understand that the visit extended at least some number of days and likely included at least some basic instruction of the new converts. In the midst of such daily exhortation, a new trouble arose:

> It happened that as we were going to the place of prayer, a slave-girl having a spirit of divination met us, who was bringing her masters much profit by fortune-telling. Following after Paul and us, she kept crying out, saying, "These men are bond-servants of the Most High God, who are proclaiming to you the way of salvation." She continued doing this for many days. But Paul was greatly annoyed, and turned and said to the spirit, "I command you in the name of Jesus Christ to come out of her!" And it came out at that very moment. (Acts 16:16-18)

Let's begin to unfold this incident by examining why Paul was "annoyed" by this young woman. His reasoning is likely complex, though similar in nature to that of Jesus when, in Mark, we read, "Whenever the unclean spirits saw Him, they would fall down before Him and shout, 'You are the Son of God!' And He earnestly warned them not to tell who He was" (Mark 3:11-12). The question persists, however: why weren't they permitted to speak the truth of Jesus' nature, the revelation of the Most High, the confirmation of Paul's testimony?

We must remember that Jesus' divinity and God's perfect plan stood on its own merits. It did not need, neither did it particularly value, the confirmation of man (though a number of men were blessed to speak truth on its behalf). Guzik says it thusly: "Didn't [Paul] appreciate the free 'advertising'? [*sic*] No, because he didn't appreciate the source, and could do quite nicely without demonic approval of his ministry. Paul knew that a man will be identified by both his friends and his enemies, and could do without a demonic 'letter of reference.'" (Guzik 2001c).

Other commentators have suggested that perhaps Paul felt compassion for the young slave girl, knowing that demonic possession often meant the loss of one's agency: a lack of control over oneself, sometimes extending so far as to include harming oneself. However, the use of the word "annoyed" in this context seems to lend better credence to Guzik's interpretation. *Diaponeomai* (BLB 2016, Strong's G1278) in the Greek, this is the same word used in Acts 4 to describe the reaction of the Sadducees to Peter's preaching of the Gospel message. "…being greatly disturbed because they were teaching the people and proclaiming in Jesus the resurrection from the dead" (Acts 4:2). They were greatly disturbed. Synonyms include *troubled*, *displeased*, *offended*, or *pained*. All of these words suggest a more negative reaction on Paul's part.

In any case, upon speaking the name of Jesus Christ, the demon was exorcised, and the girl was set free.

Paul and Silas Imprisoned

It never ceases to be saddening that, while some react to the work of the Holy Spirit with open hearts, praise, and thanksgiving, many more react with denial and anger. Thus, it was with the masters of the young slave girl now set free by the power of Jesus Christ.

> But when her masters saw that their hope of profit was gone, they seized Paul and Silas and dragged them into the market place before the authorities, and when they had brought them to the chief magistrates, they said, "These men are throwing our city into confusion, being Jews, and are proclaiming customs which it is not lawful for us to accept or to observe, being Romans."
> The crowd rose up together against them, and the chief magistrates tore their robes off them and proceeded to order them to be beaten with rods. When they had struck them with many blows, they threw them into prison, commanding the jailer to guard them securely; and he, having received such a command, threw them into the inner prison and fastened their feet in the stocks. (Acts 16:19-24)

Now, let's be clear, because it would be easy to fall prey to the same misdirection here as the erstwhile audience to this miscarriage of justice. They were not, in fact, angry that Paul and his companions were Jews, or Christians, or that they were publicly speaking on the death and resurrection of Jesus Christ. They were angry because they "saw that their hope of profit was gone." As on the day of the crucifixion (see John 18:38-19:2 and 19:16-17), when Pilate, at the behest of an angry populace, ordered Jesus beaten, crowned with thorns, then hung upon a cross and murdered, in spite of his innocence, so, too, are our companions condemned. A mob is gathered, fear reigns, and Paul and Silas are beaten and imprisoned.

Many translations note that they were "severely flogged," that is, beaten with such intent to cause harm that, at the very least, they would have been bruised and bloodied and, at worst, may have sustained multiple broken bones, internal ruptures, and, in some cases, even been permanently disabled by the beating. Death itself was not unheard of as a result of this type of punishment. When something is taken from us, it can often be so easy to cry, "Not fair!" It can be easy to couch our anger, our hurt, and our desire for judgment in terms of righteousness and justice, as the owners of the slave girl did here. It can be easy to forget that we serve a God who tempers justice with mercy and judgment with compassion. In so forgetting, we run the risk of perpetuating the same consequences that Paul and Silas faced; perhaps not in the physical sense, but certainly our anger can carry, our words can wound, and our insatiable need to "even the score" can lead to tremendous harm.

In the face of such misery, I know I might begin to doubt the calling I had put my faith in. But not Paul. The very next verse encourages us, saying, "But about midnight Paul and Silas were praying and singing hymns of praise to God, and the prisoners were listening to them…" (Acts 16:25). Not only were these men refusing to be overcome by their circumstances, they were praising God in the midst of them! Many scholars agree that they were likely singing the Paschal (Passover) hymn referred to in Matthew 26:30 that would have included Psalms 113-118. Even more amazing, the other prisoners were listening, hearing of the glory of the Most High God through music and praise.

In Travis Cottrell's *Jesus Saves (Live)* album, Beth Moore speaks of this awe-inspiring scene, saying,

> They had been beaten half to death. I would suggest to you that they did not feel like worshiping. They made a choice. And in that moment they overcame every power of darkness.
>
> There is so much purification in persecution. When we don't have a negative force coming against us to unspoil us and to unify us, then we can just decide we're not going to worship because we don't like that song…or we're distracted by someone's outfit…or maybe we couldn't find a parking place…and we're just ticked off. So we're not gonna sing cause we're just not in the mood to sing.

And then we're reminded of a couple of guys torn to shreds, who lifted up their voices in the midst of so much pain. Sometimes, you praise first…and you feel it later. (Cottrell 2009)

So often, our choice to worship in the midst of great trial becomes the linchpin of God's work. Our act of faith, our decision to trust Him, *no matter what*, to trust in His plan and in His process, even when all seems lost, becomes the hinge on which God's work goes from good to Godly. It is the act of faithful worship in the face of insurmountable persecution that, like Abraham's faithfulness in being willing to sacrifice Isaac on the altar, allows the divinity and power of God to pour forth.

The Jailer Converted

As Paul and Silas chose to worship in that dark and dank cellar, locked away, bruised, bloodied, beaten, cold and naked, feet in stocks, bodies hunched in pain, the damp seeping into muscles abused beyond words, God moved: "And suddenly there came a great earthquake, so that the foundations of the prison house were shaken; and immediately all the doors were opened and everyone's chains were unfastened" (Acts 16:26).

The chains were not *broken, shattered, crushed,* or *snapped.* Nor were the doors thrown from their hinges by the percussive force. The doors were "opened" (BLB 2016, Strong's G455) as the visiting magi "opened" their treasures for Jesus (Matthew 2:11), as heaven "opened" at the baptism of Jesus (Matthew 3:16), as the door "opens" when we seek and knock (Matthew 7:7), as eyes are "opened" to the presence and power of Jesus (Matthew 9:30). Likewise, the chains were unfastened. Literally, *loosened* (BLB 2016, Strong's G447). The chains becoming unbound was not a direct result of the earthquake, of the shattering weight and power of rock and stone, but one of divine import alone. It was God who stretched forth and loosed the chains binding the prisoners. Yet, as with all miracles, they are not performed for the purposes of man (though they might do that, as well), but are to testify to the almighty power of God.

> When the jailer awoke and saw the prison doors opened, he drew his sword and was about to kill himself, supposing that the prisoners had escaped. But Paul cried out with a loud voice, saying, "Do not harm yourself, for we are all here!" And he called for lights and rushed in, and trembling with fear he fell down before Paul and Silas, and after he brought them out, he said, "Sirs, what must I do to be saved?" They said, "Believe in the Lord Jesus, and you will be saved, you and your household." And they spoke the word of the Lord to him together with all

who were in his house. And he took them that very hour of the night and washed their wounds, and immediately he was baptized, he and all his household. And he brought them into his house and set food before them, and rejoiced greatly, having believed in God with his whole household. (Acts 16:27-34)

God's hand did not move merely to free Paul and Silas. It did not move in a divine act of mercy towards those other prisoners sharing cells and stocks with our companions. It moved solely for His glory.

It is important to understand that the Jailer was not simply some night guard. Meaning *keeper of the prison* (BLB 2016, Strong's G1200), he would be more akin to a modern Warden, responsible for the security of the entire prison as well as for the implementation of justice, including beatings and, possibly, even executions. He would have been a man of the Roman administrative structure, likely a former soldier, and most assuredly, according to *Easton's Bible Dictionary*, "a man belonging to a class 'insensible as a rule and hardened by habit, and also disposed to despise the Jews, who were the bearers of the message of the gospel.'" (Easton 1897b).

Yet, this is the man who, upon hearing Paul's assurance that not a single prisoner had fled (and by what miracle had Paul even heard his lament, we might ask), responded by falling down before them and asking how to be saved. God's hand had moved; Paul had remained steadfast and obedient, with a heart positioned in worship and praise rather than selfish fear and pain; and another convert was won for the Kingdom.

And such a convert! Like Lydia, the Jailer would have brought a prestigious sphere of influence. From the prisoners committed to his care to the citizens he protected, his social standing and reputation would have ensured that his conversion would ripple across all of Philippi. We are told little else of his story beyond this point, but it might be safe to thus extrapolate his impact on Philippi and its surrounding environs.

Finally, it would be impossible to continue without drawing attention to a certain symbolic symmetry contained herein. "And he took them that very hour and washed their wounds, and immediately he was baptized, he and all his household" (Acts 16:33). As he washes their physical wounds, gently cleansing them of the blood now begriming their bodies, dried and caked, so, too, do Paul and Silas wash his spiritual wounds, baptizing him, very likely in the same water from which he drew the bucket that cleansed their own marks. It is impossible to read such a passage and not simply marvel at the depth of interpretation that the divine Word of God imbues!

Departing Philippi

While the power and providence of Paul's divine appointment with the jailer cannot be overstated, it would be unwise to forget the circumstances that initially led to his imprisonment. No matter how good intentioned, and God-intentioned, the outcome, Paul still had to deal with the complex legal ramifications of his detainment.

Paul Released

The history of Roman Jews is convoluted, to say the least. While the Jewish religion was considered *religio licita* (permitted religion) (Smallwood 2001, 539) under Julius Caesar and Augustus, by the time of Paul's visit to Philippi, relations were heavily strained; and within a few years of his writing the Book of Philippians, the Roman Empire would officially be at war with Jerusalem. Nevertheless, Paul was both a Jew and a Roman citizen, granting him specific rights beneath the auspices of the Roman government. Christians, whether converted Jews or Gentiles, meanwhile, were rarely granted either religious freedom or political power, though they might, like Paul, retain their Roman citizenship, which only serves to further muddle the conversation.

Paul's citizenship originated with his birth in Tarsus, a free city of Rome, and, thus, ensured that he was both born a Roman and remained a Roman citizen, despite his Jewish inheritance and his choice to follow Jesus. In fact, Paul leveraged his Roman citizenship on a number of occasions. Acts 22 shows us both why and how this was a powerful bargaining tool under Roman authority.

> But when they stretched him out with thongs, Paul said to the centurion who was standing by, "Is it lawful for you to scourge a man who is a Roman and uncondemned?" When the centurion heard this, he went to the commander and told him, saying, "What are you about to do? For this man is a Roman." The commander came and said to him, "Tell me, are you a Roman?" And he said, "Yes." The commander answered, "I acquired this citizenship with a large sum of money." And Paul said, "But I was actually born a citizen." (Acts 22:25-28)

Interestingly, this scene illustrates only one of a number of times that Paul was to be beaten, imprisoned, or wrongfully treated, but is the first to highlight his efforts to avoid such action. Why, then, knowing this, did Paul suffer himself to be beaten and imprisoned in Acts 16? Perhaps for the same reasons that, unlike Peter in Acts 12:3-11, Paul did not make good his escape from the crumbling prison: a greater service was to be performed by remaining. While Peter would surely have died a martyr, Paul would have missed the opportunity to preach to the Jailer and his family. In short, Peter *went* by the Hand of God; Paul, likewise, *stayed*. (Incidentally, it is important to note that, unlike Paul, Peter was not a Roman citizen, and, therefore, not entitled to the protections Paul describes in this verse.)

Returning to Philippi, however, we discover that while Paul did not prevent his trials through declaring his citizenship, he nevertheless leveraged its not insignificant power on the morning after the Jailer's conversion.

> Now when day came, the chief magistrates sent their policemen, saying, "Release those men." And the jailer reported these words to Paul, saying, "The chief magistrates have sent to release you. Therefore come out now and go in peace." But Paul said to them, "They have beaten us in public without trial, men who are Romans, and have thrown us into prison; and now are they sending us away secretly? No indeed! But let them come themselves and bring us out." The policemen reported these words to the chief magistrates. They were afraid when they heard that they were Romans, and they came

and appealed to them, and when they had brought them out, they kept begging them to leave the city. They went out of the prison and entered the house of Lydia, and when they saw the brethren, they encouraged them and departed. (Acts 16:35-40)

While the text can clearly speak for itself, we are left to wonder, again, *why*? Not only why Paul chose not to reveal his legal rights prior to being beaten, which we've already answered, but also, why reveal it at all, then, at this point? This is where my heart thrills for Paul and his political savvy. Paul was not merely a teacher and evangelizer, he was also a very wise and astute man, intelligent, well-educated, and erudite, which we will delve into more deeply later. On the one hand, remaining silent, likely at the behest of the Holy Spirit, yielded the powerful conversion of the Jailer and his family. On the other hand, however, is the political shrewdness likely born and bred into him from his youngest years.

Paul was preparing to leave Philippi. He was well aware that he had outstayed his welcome and that nothing more would come of his remaining but further chaos and confusion. By withdrawing, he allowed his enemies a sense of victory, but the sense only, not the substance, as he had already converted to Christ at least two of the preeminent citizens of the city. He also laid the foundation for their own future defense. He understood that Christians would be persecuted, had experienced this firsthand, and so he laid his final card, an ace. In waiting until after the offense against his citizenship had already been committed, Paul used it as an object example for how Christian Roman citizens ought to react and was able to do so in a highly public manner. In Colossians, Paul writes, "When He had disarmed the rulers and authorities, He made a public display of them, having triumphed over them through Him" (Colossians 2:15). While these words were in regard to Christ's death on the cross, I think a similar argument could hold true here, in Philippi. Paul left, not quietly, as he informs the Jailer, but for all to see: a humiliating lesson for the Roman authority in Philippi, an encouraging one for those who might soon face a similar persecution, and a triumphant departure from the very first European Church.

Completing The Journey

While our course of study primarily concentrates here, in this place, on this particular, God-ordained stop, it would be unwise to forget the remainder of our companions' journey, given the extent to which it will inform our understanding of the Book of Philippians. Suffice it to say that after a stay of several days to weeks in Philippi, Paul departed and continued on towards Thessalonica. Here, the pattern repeated: the arrival of Paul to preach in the gathering place first of the Jews, then also reaching out to the Gentiles, followed by a number of converts, then the jealous inciting of a mob and the eventual eviction of our travelers (Acts 17:1-9). Thence, to Berea where, again, the pattern is followed (Acts 17:10-15). Departing Berea alone, Paul continued on to Athens where, waiting for Silas and Timothy, he again shared the Gospel in the famed *Sermon on Mars Hill* (Acts 17:22-31). Next, Paul and his companions set forth to Corinth, where they remained for almost a year and a half (Acts 18:1-17). Finally, Paul departed Corinth and set out for Syria, then to Ephesus, and, from there, he returned to the brethren in Antioch (Acts 18:18-22).

All told, this journey likely lasted somewhere in the vicinity of five years, from 49CE to 54CE, and constituted over 3,000 miles of travel (www.openbible.info 2012), most of which was executed on foot. Given that this was only one of four missionary journeys that Paul embarked upon, it is easy to see his devotion to both the spreading of the Gospel message as well as his passion for those churches that were created in the wake of his visits. Indeed, much of his later ministry may not even have been possible without this journey, as this was the one that opened the initial doors into the Roman Empire, and, as we will see as we enter into our study of Philippians, progressed so far as to have infiltrated the highest levels of the government by the time of its writing around 62CE.

Paul's Personal Journey

Luke includes many descriptions of the power of God and the movement of the Holy Spirit in his writing of Acts. Nevertheless, it is easy to become trapped by the narrative style and fall prey to the deception that it is nothing more than a recounting of the early events of the Church. Clearly, the Spirit of God was at work, moving Paul, Timothy, Silas, and sometimes, Luke himself, to the rhythm of His providential plan. In so doing, not only were the lives of those to whom Paul ministered being changed, but Paul's, too, must have been greatly impacted by his work.

As a young college student, my husband and I were blessed to do a medical missions trip to a small clinic in rural Kenya. He, growing up within the Church, had been on many such trips before. For me, though, it was a first. To this day, over a decade later, the impact of those six weeks is hard to describe. On the one hand, like Luke, I can tell the story of those days and weeks like they have only just happened. I remember the names of the patients we worked with: Timothy, Peter, Margaret; I know the incredible power of life we were giving to them. Yet, when I dig deeper, past the outward simplicity of the narration of our trip to the deep, spiritual truths that God was imparting to me during that time, the details become hazy.

Was it then that I became passionate for the causes of poverty, medical care, mobility, and education? Or were the seeds simply planted, neither to grow nor flourish until God's divine hand had guided me through other experiences, which watered and fertilized those carefully sown crops? The truth is, I was probably my own worst enemy for the duration of the trip and spent less time pursuing God than I did my own pride of place.

I'd like to believe that Paul's heart was different. Indeed, to have embarked on a journey such as this one, it must have been. Like modern missionaries who spend months preparing to enter the field and years living abroad in an attempt to make an impact for the Kingdom, it is hard to believe that Paul might have had anything other than a firm reliance upon God's favor.

Nevertheless, we must remember Paul's mindset as he set out from Antioch: Barnabas gone, alone and feeling betrayed, finding his way with a new partner, and, all the while, making every effort to seek and glorify God to the best of his ability. I can't help but wonder what Paul learned of himself on this journey.

Because it is *this* self, the one he finds during this and his subsequent journeys, that so informs and impacts his later writings to those churches generated by his visits: Philippians, 1 & 2 Thessalonians, and 1 & 2 Corinthians, all of which exude a paternal love and filial obligation akin to a father looking after his beloved children. What, then, changed, to bring the fiery, passionate, strong-willed young man of Acts 15 to the astute and venerated father figure of Acts 28?

I think, as with all spiritual matters, the answer is both simple and complex: God. I think that Paul accepted Jesus, accepted – outwardly, at least – the mantle of his calling, very early on. Nevertheless, he writes ceaselessly of his need to lay himself aside, to fully succumb to the power of Christ in him, to count all as lost in light of the saving grace of Jesus. I don't think he would write so passionately of these things if he had not, himself, been forced to internalize them at some point.

Paul was a man of pride and passion and power. The divine appointment of his conversion notwithstanding, the internalization of his humility, meekness, and service must have been a challenge. Indeed, he makes no secret of that fact. Why else, then, would God see fit to send "a thorn in the flesh, a messenger of Satan to torment me—to keep me from exalting myself!" (2 Corinthians 12:7)? Upon imploring the Lord to remove said thorn, God even counseled Paul, "My grace is sufficient for you, for [my] power is perfected in weakness," (2 Corinthians 12:9).

Paul's journey may have been undertaken for the glory of God and the extension of His kingdom, but I believe that it was during this journey, in some unnamed corner on a quiet city block or on the open road, dust coating his feet and filling his mouth, or, most likely, in the midst of the many persecutions that he faced in these five years, that Paul met God in a new and exciting way, fully inhabiting the spirit within him and fully allowing that Spirit to inhabit him, then pouring outward in a virtual manifestation of fire and power, in the Name of the Most High.

Introducing Philippians

As Christians, I think we always yearn to learn more. The mysteries of God and His Holy Spirit, of the resurrection of Jesus Christ, of the portents and end times are a siren's lure, particularly in our age of enlightenment, to ever ask, "How can I go deeper?" At its heart, there is a danger here. Solomon cautions,

> But beyond this, my son, be warned: the writing of many books is endless, and excessive devotion to books is wearying to the body. The conclusion, when all has been heard, is: fear God and keep His commandments, because this applies to every person. For God will bring every act to judgment, everything which is hidden, whether it is good or evil. (Ecclesiastes 12:12-14).

Yet, the Bible was written to be understood within certain contexts: historical, cultural, and social contexts that have long since shifted with the passage of time and epochs. How, then, can we fully comprehend that which has been endowed to us without constantly seeking a deeper understanding of both the world in which it was originally penned and the lives of those who were setting pen to page? While a cursory reading of the Bible will, no doubt, yield a harvest of spiritual truths, it is only through further study that we begin to see the richness of God's tapestry. As our understanding of Paul's visit to Philippi in Acts was enhanced by better comprehending the historical, social, and political climate of the day, so, too, will our journey through Philippians be more thoroughly informed by additional background knowledge.

Commentators typically agree that any Biblical introduction ought to include a basic awareness of several fields of study. Who wrote it, where it was written, when it was written, and why it was written are some of the most important. These questions can sometimes have very straightforward answers, as with many of Paul's letters, where his authorship is clearly defined by his greeting or closings. On the contrary, many Old Testament books still lack definitive authorial resolution. Sometimes, as we will see with Philippians, there might be several possible answers, with both historians and commentators engaging in lively debate as to the pros and cons of each option. In short, we are given to know some of God's mysteries and not given to know others. I think it reminds us of the humility of our human condition and the extravagant omniscience of God that, try as we might, we still lack definitive answers to even some of the most basic questions of Biblical study.

Who?

Fortunately, Philippians is one that lacks any authorial debate. It is clearly and decidedly a letter of Paul by way of Timothy's scribing. Philippians, itself, gives the most conclusive evidence of this fact, beginning, "Paul and Timothy, bond-servants of Christ Jesus" (Philippians 1:1). Paul includes Timothy as a mark of humility and respect for a fellow laborer who had toiled alongside him in serving the church at Philippi. A mere scribe might not have merited inclusion; the young man who has become as a son to Paul most certainly did. It is worth noting, too, that a number of later authors attribute Philippians to Paul, and two early canonical collections, the Muratorian Canon and the Special Canon of Marcion, both include Philippians and credit its authorship to Paul (Herrick 2004).

Where and When?

Unfortunately, the question of the authorship of Philippians is just about the only one that has been definitively answered. Both the where and the when are a bit more problematic and enter into those scholarly debates that were mentioned earlier. If written in this place, then it must have been at such-and-such a time, but if this time, then it must have been such-and-such a place. And so it goes. The two are inextricably bound, and the greatest clue for both lies midway through the first chapter, when Paul refers to his ongoing imprisonment (yes, he has again been imprisoned as he writes his letter to the church at Philippi). This, at least, allows us to narrow the possible dates and locations to only those places in which he had been imprisoned and under Praetorian Guard, which is specifically referred to in Philippians 1:13. While we will further explore the significance of both of these topics later on, for now, it is enough to know that Paul is writing from a Roman prison. But which one?

    The answer to this question is, as yet, a source of scholarly debate. Three prevailing theories, however, seem most likely. The first theory states the location of authorship to be in Rome, while the date of authorship is likely around 62CE. This would place it concurrent with the events described in Acts 28:30 and following. While there are a number of logistical challenges to this theory, including the distance between Rome and Philippi and the prevalence of travel between the two locations; nevertheless, it remains the most likely.

The two other theories place the location and date of writing in Ephesus around 54CE (see Acts 19) and in Caesarea around 60CE (see Acts 24). The Ephesus hypothesis was generated in order to address the issues of travel within the Roman theory, as well as because of Paul's reference in Philippians to his trouble with Judaizers, which would concur with the account of Acts 19. However, it has little more to recommend it, and there is no record of Paul ever having been imprisoned in Ephesus. Likewise, the Caesarean theory is complicated by the same travel concerns as the Roman one, with nothing more to substantiate it than a written record of Paul's imprisonment therein (Zondervan 2014).

Perhaps it is most important, then, to note that God does not always give us all the answers. Perhaps it is, indeed, a lesson in humility. Perhaps it is simply because they are not needed. Certainly, in this case, knowing which theory prevails might give us some added insight, but lacking confirmation hardly shatters the foundation of our understanding of Philippians. Whether in Rome, Ephesus, or Caesarea, whether 54CE, 60CE, or 62CE, the locations, the time, and the historical, cultural, and social complexities of the day would have been similar enough that the specifics become somewhat moot.

Of course, a complete understanding of Philippians must take into account the assumption made herein that Philippians is, in fact, a single work. Some commentators continue to believe that it is a disparity of works, totaling as many as three separate letters, later conjoined into one whole. While no true consensus currently exists on any of these topics, we shall simply accept the premise that the simplest answer is the most likely and continue in our assumption that this was a Roman imprisonment around 60-62CE, which, incidentally, would put this writing congruent with approximately Acts 24:27 and following.

Finally, and perhaps more important than any of this academic debate, it would behoove any serious Bible scholar to make note of the chronological location of the book they are studying. The question of "When?" in relation to other books within the New Testament is vitally important to understand, as we will see. In the case of Philippians, it is widely believed to be the eighth New Testament book to be written, preceded by James (50CE), 1 and 2 Thessalonians (50-52CE), Galatians (55CE), 1 and 2 Corinthians (57CE), and Romans (57-58CE). It is immediately followed by Colossians, Philemon, and Ephesians, which were all written around the same time (or possible concurrently with

Philippians) in 62-63CE (assuming our Roman provenance from above).

Interestingly, the first Gospel was not written until 63CE. The four Gospel accounts, encompassing the first four books of the New Testament, so inform our modern perception of Paul's letters that it can often be hard to comprehend a time in which they did not exist. The lens through which we interpret the New Testament, the written recording of the life and times of Jesus Christ and his redemptive act on the Cross, simply did not exist. While we, as modern readers, might read Philippians and nod sagely as we see how it fits into the larger narrative of Christ's death and resurrection, readers (or, more likely, hearers) within the early church would have had to place their faith fully in Paul's interpretation of those events. Put another way, understanding this concept completely flips the perspective: we often read the New Testament as a guide for the enacting of our faith, made complete in Jesus Christ; they would have heard it as a framework of faith, informing the actions Paul had already encouraged them to take.

In order to better understand the monumental shift in perspective this invites, let's peek ahead.

> Have this attitude in yourselves which was also in Christ Jesus, who, although He existed in the form of God, did not regard equality with God a thing to be grasped, but emptied

> Himself, taking the form of a bond-servant, and being made in the likeness of men. Being found in appearance as a man, He humbled Himself by becoming obedient to the point of death, even death on a cross. For this reason also, God highly exalted Him, and bestowed on Him the name which is above every name, so that at the name of Jesus every knee will bow, of those who are in heaven and on earth and under the earth, and that every tongue will confess that Jesus Christ is Lord, to the glory of God the Father. (Philippians 2:5-11)

A more concise gospel message would be hard to find within the Scriptures. While Paul could wax poetic, and often garnished his prose with flourishes of metaphor difficult for even the most seasoned of scholars to follow, the brevity of these verses is intentional. The simple facts of Christ's deity, death, resurrection, and exaltation are laid plainly forth, a gospel message wholly independent of the 89 chapters and innumerable verses that are encompassed in Matthew, Mark, Luke, and John. Paul, in essence, is laying a foundation for their faith which did not depend on knowledge of the extensive history of Jesus' life, a knowledge that we rely on today, sometimes to a detrimental extent.

Perhaps it would behoove each of us, then, to have so simple a faith as what Paul describes here. As Solomon said, "fear God and keep His commandments" (Ecclesiastes 12:13).

Why?

The final question we must answer before delving into Philippians is, perhaps, more consuming. *Why* did Paul write this letter? What had occurred, what movement of the Spirit prompted him, what lesson did he mean to impart with its inscription? I believe that the answer to this question is both layered and nuanced.

On the surface, Paul has written perhaps the original Missionary Update Letter. Similar to our modern missionaries, Paul has received a gift of funds from the church at Philippi and wishes to express his gratitude for their partnership in the spreading of the gospel. Through this lens, Philippians can read almost as any other missions field update, including a thank you, an update on the work of the gospel, an exhortation to faithfulness, and a reminder of the glory of God.

Nevertheless, to go no deeper would deprive any serious reader of the complexities of the letter at hand. Yes, Paul was writing in thanks to Philippi for their gift and their faithfulness. But Paul was also writing to share with them the tender heart he held towards them, warranted, it seems, by his accounting of their deeds, their resolute and sincere faith, and, most importantly, their commitment to the truth of Jesus' resurrection that had been shared with them.

It is interesting to note that in 1 Thessalonians (which, you will remember, pre-dated the writing of Philippians by nearly 10 years) Paul says, "…but after we had already suffered and been mistreated in Philippi, as you know…" (1 Thessalonians 2:2). His remembrance of them, then, was hardly an untarnished one, yet commentators widely agree that so uplifting and encouraging is Philippians that it is aptly nicknamed *The Book of Joy*. How, then, does such a thing come to pass? Paul had been beaten and wrongfully imprisoned, treated shamefully, and yet, his letter to the church therein overflows with love. What took place in the eleven years or so since his visit that so shifted his perception of his time there?

I think that Paul's heart rings true throughout Philippians. It was not the events of his time there that are his most precious and cherished memories, but the people. And it is to these same people that he writes so passionately. Paul begins Philippians by saying, "We give thanks to God always for all of you…" (Philippians 1:2). For *all of you*. Paul goes on to say that he prays for each of them as well. Not one person in the church at Philippi is forgotten by Paul. Each and every one holds a special place in his heart. What a beautiful reflection of the incredibly intimate love of God for each of us! Each name is known, each prayer is uplifted, personalized and profound, each face is remembered with love and tenderness. As Paul saw himself a father to the early churches he had planted, so too does he demonstrate the Father's love for each of us.

To return to our question, then, of *why* Paul wrote this letter, it is clear that it was written not simply in gratitude, but as a personal confirmation of Paul's deep and abiding love for the citizens of Philippi. It is a letter of encouragement – the only one, in fact, in which no chastisement is offered to the established church (Henry 1706b). It is a letter of joy, with that word appearing some 16 times in only four chapters. It is a letter between dear friends, separated by distance, but held close in spirit and in faith.

Themes of Philippians

As with the questions of *where* and *when*, identifying the common themes within Philippians is also problematic. Many commentators disagree on what these themes may be, or even that there is a cohesive theme throughout (leading to the theory that Philippians was originally more than one letter, later conjoined, which has largely been discredited by the academic community, today). At best, the majority of commentators are content to write a basic outline, especially as Philippians is so personal a letter from Paul that it has almost a stream-of-consciousness air to it, flitting rapidly between subjects. Most agree that it includes exhortations to remain faithful, even in the midst of near-certain persecution and the presence of many false teachers. It also serves to commend both Timothy and Epaphroditus to the church at Philippi. Interestingly, these two themes may be intertwined, as it serves the critically important role of establishing their authority and credentials to an early church both rife with false teachers and wholly dependent upon itinerant preachers for their further education.

Some of the more common suggestions for a theme include the idea of joy or rejoicing, even in difficult circumstances; a vigorous and active in-living of the Holy Spirit, leading to an understanding of the importance of a good and Godly attitude; and the idea of the importance of community and fellowship within the church and its necessity to the individual Christian. The *NIV Study Bible* goes on to say of Philippians, "It contains one of the most profound Christological passages in the [New Testament] (2:5–11). Yet, profound as it is, Paul includes it mainly for illustrative purposes" (Barker 2014). Of course, we have already looked at this passage, and will again before we are finished.

Nevertheless, most commentators list the overarching themes of Philippians in terms of the general placement of various topics throughout the letter: thanksgiving for their gift to him, a report on his own circumstances, exhortations to humility and fellowship, his faith in Timothy and

Epaphroditus, and his warning against those who might try to lead them astray. On the whole, it reads more as a framework than a thematic study.

Robert Swift, on the other hand, suggests that Philippians is, indeed, thematically written and applied, pointing to Philippians 1:3-6 for his hypothesis. He states,

> Verses 3-6, then, are a cameo of the entire epistle. They introduce the main theme, the Philippians' partnership in the gospel. This theme is developed in the direction of God's perfecting of both them and their works for the gospel. All the rest of the letter is concerned primarily with their development as [partners] so that they may be blessed with a temporally fruitful, eternally rewardable [*sic*] partnership in the gospel. (Swift 1984)

He believes, then, that the theme is this: the Philippians' partnership in the gospel.

Arguably, any of these could encompass the purpose of Paul's letter to the church at Philippi. However, as we read the Bible through the twin lenses of our modern perceptions and our current trials, I think it more important to note that any scholarly quest into the themes of Philippians ought to be of less concern than what we, the readers, might glean of Paul's wisdom. As I studied the book of Philippians with an eye to my audience of women, perhaps the exhortations to unity and fellowship seemed most important at the time.

Rereading it in preparation to write to a wholly different audience, I find different themes clamoring for attention. The danger, again, in seeking too deeply the scholarly nature of the Bible is that we miss the personal, intimate messages that God has prepared for our ears, alone.

There are some interesting, additional notes, too, when it comes to Philippians – not themes, per se, but worth taking the time to acknowledge before we delve more deeply into its message. Philippians is one of a number of books in the New Testament that does not include any Old Testament quotations. Nearly one third of the 27 New Testament books share this quality (1 & 2 Thessalonians, Philippians, Colossians, Titus, Philemon, Jude, and 1-3 John), with more than half of those being written by Paul. This might help account for Paul's recognition as "missionary to the Gentiles," despite his well-documented tendency towards visiting the local synagogue first. For a Jew among Jews, as we shall see, he was remarkably sensitive to the cultural biases of his audience, not resorting to Old Testament scripture where it would clearly lack authority or credibility. Nevertheless, Philippians does contain a number of allusions to the Old Testament and to the cultural beliefs of any Judaic readers.

Additionally, it is important to remember that Philippians was written near the same time as Colossians,

Philemon, and Ephesians, so concurrent themes between these books also exist. It might be wise, in fact, to consider reading each of those letters together with Philippians, or directly afterwards, to get a clear picture of the wider cultural, social, and religious issues that Paul was addressing at this point in history.

Remember, 11 years have passed between the events of Philippi and the penning of this letter. The entirety of Acts 16-24 has already occurred. Paul can now look back on his time in Philippi as the origination of his call not only to Europe, but also to the Gentiles of the Roman Empire and see the rich tapestry of God's providential hand in each and every assignation from then until now. It is a beautiful illustration of divine appointments, extreme hardship, and souls won in Jesus' name. From prison, he writes to the city of his first imprisonment of what he has learned of God's incredible provision and the joy one can find in His presence, even in the worst circumstances imaginable. Paul has grown up, as has the little congregation in Philippi; they stand together, across time and distance, to speak their words to us, today, who would hear them.

A Moment to Reflect

It has now been more than six months since I sat in a small, local café and decided to embark on a study of Philippians. As I've made this journey, I can't help but be in awe of the providence that God not only showed Paul, but also that which He shows me. That dark, cloudy, Seattle-grey day, as I tried to juggle my toddler, a Bible, a notebook, and a very serious conversation about what we ought to spend our precious few weeks covering, I remember blurting out, "I've always loved Philippians." It is with amazement that I look back and realize the import of that moment, and the way in which it has changed the trajectory of my life in ways I could not have then imagined.

I've always been a public speaker with a passion for teaching; I have not always been a committed Biblical scholar. I love to read and to learn, but my heart has not always been for God's Word. Somehow, I thought these things would come naturally, as a corollary to having become a Christian. That they hadn't seemed to speak more to my areas of interest and expertise, my *gifts*, if you will, than any lack of discipline on my part. It has only been in the last few years, as I've tried to diligently pursue God's Word and adequately prepare for its sharing, that I've come to realize that Biblical scholarship, even simply the act of sitting down to read one's Bible, is a practice one must actively engage in. I say *practice* very deliberately, because the word connotes not just the activity in question, but also the diligent, daily, disciplined drive to pursue it. Who among us would assume that taking a tennis class will make us a star player? Or that taking a piano class will make us a star performer? So, too, with our Bible. We embrace the death and resurrection of Jesus Christ and are saved, but how is it that we then think our mere attendance at church is enough to make us Biblical scholars? Paul says, "For I am confident of this very thing, that He who began a good work in you will perfect it until the day of Christ Jesus" (Philippians 1:6). The "big work" of salvation has been accomplished, but the small works, the perfection of our faith, is yet to be attained. That will only come through a practice of those things which we are called to do.

    I think it would be presumptuous of me to claim that my journey has in any way reflected Paul's. Yet, I don't think it would be so far a stretch as to suggest that, perhaps, his journey inspired my own. I thought to join Paul in Philippians, but he would not let me. Instead, by the Holy Spirit, I was sent to Acts 16. Even then, when it came time to put to paper that which I had eagerly shared with our small women's group, I was sent even farther afield, from the opening chapters of Acts, then clear to James. As these pages have grown and expanded, and in my own current study of the Old Testament, I find myself jotting verses in the corners of notes: Ecclesiastes, 1 Kings, Job, and Jonah. Meanwhile, my careful study of Paul has led me to feel the intimacy and sweet fellowship of his words, and I can hardly wait to return to the New Testament, where I know Colossians and Ephesians await my attention. For a girl who used to struggle to read only a few verses, this all-encompassing love for the Word is a euphoric surprise.

There are moments when I struggle to put to words the revelation shown me by the Holy Spirit. Perhaps, when we arrive there, I will, by the grace of God, be given the ability to express the power of Philippians 2:12-13: the in-working of Christ, the out-working of the Holy Spirit, alive within us, perfecting us daily. The truth that it is not ours to do, but an act of God, already being done within us. Two verses that revolutionized my entire concept of working out my faith, and may He give me words to adequately explain that which He has lain on my heart.

There are moments when I know there is deeper meaning, deeper truth, but just beyond my grasp. After studying the fire of the Old Testament altar and the symbolism of the fire pouring forth from heaven and settling upon those waiting on the Holy Spirit on the day of Pentecost, it is hard to read 1 Kings 18:38 – where the Lord's divine fire devoured not only Elijah's offering, but the very altar itself, and a deep trench of water besides – and not realize that there is some profound spiritual truth therein that seems just out of reach. I shall have to study more.

Finally, there are moments when my own providential appointments are kept. My family raises and trains service dogs. Recently an individual wholly outside of our Christian circles approached me with a number of questions about how to train her own dog to meet some of her needs. After days of research, she and I met to discuss her options. Is it ironic, then, that at church the very next Sunday, both at a different service and in a different spot than is our usual, I sat next to a foster mom who was struggling to meet the exact same challenges with one of the little girls who had been placed in her home? Or was it divinely appointed that I already had at my fingertips every resource she needed? Oh, heavenly Father, let me never again assume that Your will cannot be wrought, even when it seems in every way wholly disconnected from my walk with You.

I wonder if Paul felt the same rush of excitement as he saw the Lord work. I wonder if his heart quickened, if his lips couldn't help but speak, if his spirit within him thrilled with each new discovery of the Lord's faithfulness and power. I wonder if he couldn't wait to share God's proved promises with his companions, as I cannot wait to tell my dearest friends when the Lord stands firm and proves Himself in my life.

I wonder, too, if there are moments that he held close, refusing to write about them, even years later, as Mary did with her infant Savior, "pondering them in her heart" (Luke 2:19). There are still, small, silent things that I share with no one: promises God has made to me that I walk in faith He will fulfill; truths He has shown me that I believe, no matter what others might say; special blessings that He has granted me, meaningless to others, but so intimately and carefully designed to delight me that I know He has had His hand on them. I can't help but wonder what Paul's still, small, silent truths were, that he shared with no one except God.

Indeed, we have not yet even reached our study of the Book of Philippians, and I could write another dozen chapters before reaching our end goal. Yet, I will resist. Perhaps there will be other opportunities. Perhaps those are for another person yet to write. Perhaps we shall journey together again, as Paul and Timothy so often did.

In any case, I invite you now to put this book aside for a moment. As we will spend the next several chapters delving deep into the heart of Philippians, I encourage you, now, if you have not already done so, to go to your Bible. In the academic field, we call this a *primary source*: a document that was written or created during the specific time we are studying. The Bible ought always to be your primary source when it comes to any Biblical study; and, while interpretation may vary from commentator to commentator (typically called a *secondary source)*, it is important to remember that the Word of God is immutable. In Hebrews, the writer warns, "Jesus Christ is the same yesterday and today and forever. Do not be carried away by varied and strange teachings…" (Hebrews 13:8-9). How do we know, then, what is strange or varied? We return, again, to the Bible, itself, God's proof of his good and perfect Word and will.

So, with this in mind, go to your Bible, your translation of choice, and read the book of Philippians. The whole thing? Yes, if you will. It is only four short chapters, and our study herein will be all the richer for having done so. Go ahead; we'll wait for you. As you do so, I invite you to consider not only the common themes that we've already discussed, but also to listen for the still, small voice of the Lord as He speaks intimately to your spirit. When you've done so, please join us here, again, as we begin to study God's Word, through Paul, to the Church at Philippi.

Grace to You and Peace

For fear that this might simply become just another commentary, my hope over the next few chapters will be to avoid over-spiritualizing the obvious and instead settle for a philosophy of "going deeper." In this vein, my goal is to provide historical background and word usage study that should enhance your understanding of Philippians without presuming to be any kind of theological scholar. Where it is necessary, of course, we will draw the appropriate spiritual parallels; but my hope is not to commentate, but rather to invite a more intimate knowledge of Paul and the Church at Philippi, as well as the unique challenges that were present at the time that this letter was written.

Before we begin, then, please return to your Bible and re-read Philippians 1:1-11. As you do so, please join me in praying:

Heavenly Father, we ask that you would come into our study today and in all the days to follow. We ask that, by the Holy Spirit, You would move. That You would reveal spiritual truths, that You would speak revelation, and that You would meet those who knock upon the door of wisdom, opening it wide and inviting us into Your sweet presence. In Your most holy Name. Amen.

Philippians 1:1a

Following the style of the day, Philippians opens almost in reverse to what we, as modern readers, would expect; this is how a letter ought to end. Nevertheless, there is a value in such an opening which invites the reader to recognize the authority by which the author writes. Perhaps, then, it is more akin to receiving a letter on personalized, monogrammed stationary, or on official letterhead, which tells us, *This is the authority by which I write to you.* What, then, was Paul's authority? His status as a bond-servant, or slave, of Christ Jesus.

But what does this mean? Today, we do not have bond-servants. Even slavery seems a distasteful concept, and with good reason, given its devastating role in American history. How, then, do we begin to understand this concept of bonded servitude?

In the Greek, *doulos* (BLB 2016, Strong's G1401) is generally translated as slave or servant, with a connotation very closely akin to our modern understanding of the word *slave*. However, it also hearkens back to a unique aspect of Jewish culture: the bond-servant, *'ebed* in the Hebrew, pronounced eh'-ved. It is in Exodus that we read the origins of this term.

> If you buy a Hebrew slave, he shall serve for six years; but on the seventh he shall go out as a free man without payment... But if the slave plainly says, "I love my master, my wife and my children; I will not go out as a free man," then his master shall bring him to God, then he shall bring him to the door or the doorpost. And his master shall pierce his ear with an awl; and he shall serve him permanently. (Exodus 21:2, 5-6)

The transaction that takes place here, between master and slave, is an intriguing earthly reflection of the spiritual manifestation of which Paul speaks. For love of his Master, Paul has called himself "bought with a price" (1 Corinthians 6:20), not just a slave, lacking the rights of personhood that we usually equate with that state, but a bond-servant, chosen of Christ and choosing, as well. What is unique about this transaction is the reciprocity it entails. A bad slave, one who was lazy, who refused to work, or who only gave his minimum effort would likely not be kept on by his master. Choosing this path, though, would mean a certain level of respect within the household, and without, as well. Indeed, it would be considered a mark of honor to have had one's ear pierced by his master, a sign of his devotion and his master's acceptance. We see a striking illustration of the kind of servant this might entail, and the kind of servant it would not, in Matthew 25:14-30, The Parable of the Talents, where the Servant given five talents multiplies his responsibility and gains honor in his Master's eyes, while the Servant given only one buries it and is disgraced. The former might merit becoming a bond-servant, if he so chose, while the latter was immediately removed.

In light of this, it is easy to understand why Paul might refer to himself as a bond-servant of Christ Jesus. Marked not in the flesh, but in the spirit, he is wholly devoted to Christ, proud to bear His mark and perform His work on Earth.

It is interesting to note, too, that this was one of several ways in which Paul referred to his relationship with Christ. While he used this same term, "bond-servant," in Romans and Titus, he also paired it with the term "apostle;" while in 1 & 2 Corinthians, Galatians, Ephesians, Colossians, and 1 & 2 Timothy, he used "apostle" alone. 1 & 2 Thessalonians lack any such descriptor, though, as used in his first letters; perhaps Paul had not yet settled on a writing style. Finally, Philemon uses the word "prisoner," perhaps in respectful recognition of the subject of that letter. In any case, Paul seems to take every opportunity to remind his readers of the subservient role that he takes before Christ and invites us to see ourselves in the same way. If Paul, that great father of the faith, can see himself in such a submissive role, so, too, should we.

Philippians 1:1b-2

In his sweeping commentary, William Barclay writes, "When Paul took and put together these two great words, grace and peace, *charis* and *eirēnē*, he…was taking the normal greeting phrases of two great nations and moulding them into one" (Barclay 1959, 15). He goes on to explain that *grace* is a very common Greek greeting, while *peace*, of course, holds great significance as the Hebrew greeting *shalom*. By combining the two, Paul created, in essence, a whole new phrase, one that would mark Christian writing for millennia to come. Grace, that concept of wholly unmerited and undeserved favor, yet granted by faith in Christ Jesus; and peace, not stagnation, as when we are still and without challenge, but holding firm, steady and steadfast in the midst of the inevitable storm. That he was the first to do so is not in question, and a casual reading of the first few verses of almost any letter of Paul's will yield this same greeting. (Only 1 & 2 Timothy differ, adding mercy, while Titus uses the same greeting, though not in the opening lines.) Barclay continues, "Each of these words had its own flavor, and each of them was intensified and deepened and made infinitely more precious by the new meaning which Christianity poured into it" (Barclay 1959, 15).

However, interesting as this word study is, what really sets these verses apart is their corporate nature. While we often read our Bibles through the lens of individual instruction, we must not forget that Paul was writing to the entire congregation at Philippi, which is specifically noted in the preceding verse. As such, it is important to understand that Paul is not only wishing grace and peace *to* the individual believers at Philippi, but also *among* the individual believers at Philippi. In short, his blessing is this: *may you be corporately gracious and peaceful with one another.* As their culture was one of community, so, too, does Paul emphasize the need to live in close harmony with each other, a theme he returned to in later chapters, with admonition to those who were not.

Philippians 1:3-6

In 1 Samuel, the titular prophet says to the people of Israel, "Moreover, as for me, far be it from me that I should sin against the Lord by ceasing to pray for you…" (1 Samuel 12:23). Paul, too, sees this as a sacred duty, often offering up more than one prayer for the congregation in his writing to them.

For years, I have struggled to pray well. I struggle to pray with intentional regularity, I struggle to utilize prayer in the midst of trials, and I struggle to remember to pray for those to whom I have promised intercession. I know a number of great prayer warriors, and I often feel shame when asking for their prayers, because I know how badly I return the favor to others. I share this because I am certain that I am not the only one for whom praying is difficult.

Paul, however, prays well. He prays often. He prays with eloquence or with simplicity, as the occasion arises. Paul prays for peace, for grace, for the anxious heart, for the unkempt mind, for the holiness of God to fill the lives of those he prays for. His prayers, then, become a template for my own. Wisdom, mercy, holiness, discernment, comfort; all of these, and more, Paul offers up to the early churches, and all of these become my own prayers when I don't seem to have the right words.

Likewise, when I struggle to remember to pray for others, Paul offers up the unique model of praying through his writing. If I cannot immediately stop and pray for the person who has requested it, I follow Paul's lead and write a letter. I include within it either my own unique prayer or use one of many offered up in the Bible to express my desire that God would move.

Perhaps you are a prayer warrior and don't need to resort to such tactics, but for me, these two tools have revolutionized my ability to pray. As Paul's letters were meant to edify and uplift the early churches, I hope that my letters, too, might serve to point the reader towards God.

Why, then, is Paul praying for the Philippians? He continues, "in view of your participation in the gospel from the first day until now" (Philippians 1:5). If you will remember from our discussion of the common themes of Philippians, Swift suggested that the single, all-encompassing theme of this book is the participation of the Philippians in the gospel. Paul's emphasis on their partnership's beginning on the "first day" points to Lydia's invitation in Acts 16:15 and continues to the very day that Paul is writing. Never have the Philippians wavered in their commitment to the gospel message or in their support of Paul, himself.

Barclay suggests that there are four partnerships that the Philippians have shared with Paul: partners in grace, partners in the work of the gospel, partners in suffering for the gospel, and partners with Christ, all of which are borne out Paul's letter to Philippi. (Barclay 1959, 21-22).

The Philippians are partners in grace, as Paul has already said, by virtue of their position as saints (v. 1:1). *Hagios* in the Greek or *kadosh* in the Hebrew, it is the word used in Leviticus 21:6, "They shall be holy to their God"

(Leviticus 21:6). The word implies a sacredness, a setting apart, as the Jewish people, themselves, were set apart from other peoples. In Christ, too, we are set apart, meant to be holy. In Colossians, Paul writes, "those who have been chosen of God, holy and beloved" (Colossians 3:12).

The Philippians are partners in the work of the gospel, as we have already seen, "from the first day until now." Their partnership in the gospel, their gift of funding to Paul, is one of the primary reasons that Paul is putting pen to paper, as we will see later.

The Philippians are partners in suffering for the gospel, as we will soon see, and they are partners with Paul, called upon to emulate his model in suffering, returning all praise and worship to Christ and finding joy in said sufferings, for His sake. Thus, will they be enabled to serve God even in the midst of their trials, as Paul, himself, has done.

The Philippians are partners with Christ, equipped and sent forth to bring the gospel message to the ends of the Earth, as was His divine will. While it is easy to assume that it was only Paul who traveled widely in the name of the gospel, we must remember the spheres of influence we discussed while reading about Paul's visit to Philippi: Lydia's spheres of influence, which would have included not only the merchant class of Philippi, but also trading partners across the region;

and the Jailer's spheres of influence, which likely extended to the local military units, assigned and reassigned across the vastness of the Roman Empire and bringing with them the stories of that dark night in a Philippian jail. To assume that it was only Paul spreading the gospel of the early church would be a fallacy that would miss the true impact and importance of such churches as that of Philippi, with all of the political and cultural importance that we've already discussed.

In light of these partnerships and the continuing commitment on the part of those at Philippi to support the gospel, it is no wonder that Paul had no admonition to share with them. In truth, his praise was so high that he wrote of his confidence in them, saying, "He who began a good work in you will perfect it." As when Paul's choice to worship while chained in the pit of a jail cell allowed God the space to work – invited it, even – so, too, does the Philippians' ongoing choice to seek after God and promote the gospel ensure that they will not be abandoned. As when Jesus said, "He who has bathed needs only to wash his feet, but is completely clean" (John 13:10), the Philippians have had the great work of salvation already accomplished; it is through their service, though, through their partnership, that they are constantly being perfected, opening the door again and again for God to work on their behalf.

Philippians 1:7-11

What sweet words Paul sends to his friends at Philippi! Because this is what they are: no mere acquaintances, not a simple flock, one among many that Paul oversees, but dear and beloved friends. There can be no doubt in reading these verses that Paul holds such a gentle and fraternal affection for those he is writing to. They are in his heart. He longs for them. Interestingly, the word *affection* has a unique meaning in the original Greek. *Splagchnon* (BLB 2016, Strong's G4698), probably from the word for spleen, means "'the bowels,' which were regarded by the Greeks as the seat of the more violent passions, by the Hebrews as the seat of the tender 'affections;' hence the word denotes 'tender mercies' and is rendered 'affections'" (Vines 1940a). Indeed, Paul's longing for them would have been as a physical ache, like one too long removed from family or close friends, yearning to be reunited, as Paul goes on to express later in his letter.

With this deep and abiding friendship in mind, is it any wonder that Paul once again lifts the Philippian Church in prayer? And such a rich and tender prayer he expresses on their behalf. "Your love may abound still more and more." "In real knowledge and all discernment." "Sincere and blameless until the day of Christ." "Filled with the fruit of righteousness." "To the glory and praise of God." Remember the corporate nature of this letter and notice the vivid texture it lends to these words. He is not simply wishing that love would abound, or increase in abundance, but that their love *for one another* would do so, through the grace and peace that he has already described on their behalf. He is not simply wishing that they would receive intelligence, but that they would receive both knowledge, which connotes basic information, and discernment, which connotes that ability to apply moral judgment and wise counsel to their knowledge.

Again, the texture and layering of these words is profound. Paul goes on, further expanding this theme by reminding the Philippians that knowledge and discernment, wisdom, as we might understand their combination, is for a purpose. "So that you may approve the things that are excellent." Indeed, their wisdom must not only be fully incorporated, but it must be applied, helping them to navigate the varied and strange teachings that they would have been receiving, perceiving through the Holy Spirit those which were of God and rejecting those teachings which were not. Their ability to stand before Christ in the day of judgment depended on it!

Not only their heavenly reward, but their earthly work was also at stake. In being wise, knowledgeable, and discerning, they would be enabled by Jesus Christ to bear fruit. Paul seems deeply invested in Jesus' parable of the vine and the branches, referring to it often with an eye towards answering what good fruit ought to look like. Here in Philippians, he calls it the "fruit of righteousness." In Galatians, he calls the fruit of the Spirit "love, joy, peace, patience, kindness, goodness, faithfulness, gentleness, and self-control" (Galatians 5:22-23). A number of parallel translations offer these alternative renderings: "charity," "long-suffering," "benignity," "fidelity," and "benevolence." In any case, Paul's purpose seems clear. These are things which ought to be reaped in a life which honors Jesus Christ, and which glorifies and praises His Heavenly Father.

The Greater Progress of the Gospel

Having sent his blessings and prayers for the Church at Philippi, Paul continued his letter by sharing a powerful story of the expansion of the gospel message. It is one that we might gloss over today, not understanding the full implications of the narrative, if we fail to perceive the vitally important socio-political role that those he described played upon the stage of ancient history. With this in mind, please return to your Bible and read Philippians 1:12-18 and take a moment to pray for the Holy Spirit to open your eyes and your heart to His words.

Philippians 1:12-14

Having begun our study of Paul and the young church at Philippi in Acts, it is impossible to overlook the symbolic analogy he draws here between his time in a Philippian prison cell and his experience, now, imprisoned in

Rome. Just as his faithfulness a decade previously produced the conversion of the Philippian Jailer, so, too, his obedience to God in his confinement is continuing to bear fruit. Further, just as his imprisonment in Philippi and the conversion of the Jailer sent ripples of influence throughout that region, so, too, did his imprisonment in Rome now ensure the same. By God's providential hand, Paul had been sent to the very heart of the Roman Empire, and his influence was being felt.

While some translations refer to it as the palace guard or the imperial guard, it is critical to understand that the Praetorian Guard to which Paul was referring was not just another divine appointment for Paul. This appointment also served to launch the gospel message into the upper echelons of Roman society, laying the foundations for the conversion of Constantine I and the whole Roman Empire nearly three centuries later. Called kingmakers, emperor-assassinators, and power brokers of the empire, the Praetorian Guard were the most ambitious and prestigious military unit of the first century.

Originally formed under Augustus in 31BCE, the Praetorian Guard was initially established as an elite, military-style protection detail for the emperor.

> Equal parts secret service, special forces and urban administrators, Rome's Praetorian

Guard was one of the ancient world's most prestigious military units. These handpicked soldiers are most famous for serving as the sworn bodyguard of the Roman ruler, but they were also used as a Jack-of-all-trades force in the service of the Empire. Guardsmen fought alongside the legions on campaign, put down uprisings, pacified rioters and served as security at gladiator shows and chariot races. As their influence grew, they also played a pivotal role in the intrigue and double-crossing that blighted imperial Rome. (Andrews 2014)

Indeed, by the time of Paul's imprisonment in Rome, they had already established themselves as the critical faction of support for any individual seeking the Emperorship, even going so far as having Emperor Caligula deposed and murdered in 41CE and placing Emperor Claudius on the throne, effectively daring the Senate to oppose their growing power. The Praetorian Guard would have been the modern-day equivalent of Delta Forces or Army Rangers, but with political aspirations of grandeur and the ability to auction the presidency to the highest bidder. Edward Gibbon writes of the power of the Prefect (or head) of the Praetorian Guard,

> The command of these favored and formidable troops soon became the first office of the empire. As the government degenerated into military despotism, the Praetorian Prefect, who in his origin had been a simple captain of the guards, was placed not

only at the head of the army, but of the finances, and even the law. (Gibbon 1776, 159)

They were extremely powerful, and no Emperor hoped to gain the office without courting their power. In Acts 27:1, Paul was delivered to them.

At the end of Acts, Paul writes, "For this reason, therefore, I requested to see you and to speak with you, for I am wearing this chain for the sake of the hope of Israel" (Acts 28:20). Likewise, in Ephesians, Paul writes, "for which I am an ambassador in chains" (Ephesians 6:20). Most commentators agree that these "chains" are not simply symbolic, but particularly relevant. They likely refer to the *halusis*, which is a short chain used to bind a prisoner to his jailer, preventing escape. Paul was literally bound to his captors; but this was a two-way street, and by God's divine providence, it allowed Paul the opportunity to spend his two years in Rome proclaiming the gospel to the eminently powerful Praetorian Guard, to which he had been assigned.

The impact of this opportunity, of course, was not lost on Paul, and it was two-fold. First, we see in Philippians 4:22 that his effect on the Praetorian Guard, like that of Lydia and the Jailer, had ripples throughout their sphere of influence. "All the saints greet you, especially those of Caesar's household" (Philippians 4:22). Perhaps the Emperor, himself, was aware of his presence in Rome. Given Paul's political acumen, it seems likely that his name would have at least been known, especially considering that his later martyrdom was at the direct behest of Emperor Nero. In any case, the emperor's household, at least, knew of him. The entire Praetorian Guard, as Paul emphasizes in Philippians 1:13, knew of Paul. The majority of them probably knew him personally, not just by reputation, as the halusis chain would have been rotated in six-hour shifts, twenty-four hours a day, three hundred and sixty-five days a year, for the entirety in Paul's two-year imprisonment in Rome. Captive audience, indeed!

Not only that, but, unthinkable as it may seem, it was because of Paul's imprisonment and his growing relationship with the Praetorian Guard that many other Christians, early believers both in Rome and farther afield, gained confidence in the gospel. If the most powerful men in the empire were hearing and believing the Word, it lent conviction and assurance to those who might have initially quailed at seeing Paul yet again imprisoned. If Paul, chained day and night to the most feared men in the empire, could continue to preach the gospel with courage and determination, so, too, could they.

Philippians 1:15-18a

So, we come to the great question of whether or not motive matters. Having confirmed to the Church at Philippi that he has continued to preach, even from his imprisonment, and not only that, but, too, his commitment to do so has encouraged and empowered believers both near and far, Paul continues directly into this discussion.

I've struggled with these verses, believing that motive does, indeed, matter. Certainly, it did in Acts 16:16-18, when, during his visit to Philippi, Paul rebuked the spirit of divination which had possessed the slave girl (leading to his Philippian imprisonment). Certainly, it seemed to in Acts 8:9-25, which recounts the story of Simon the Magician, who appeared to be interested in the gospel simply for the powers it would offer him. How, then, can Paul reach this point in his ministry and yet say, "Only that in every way, whether in pretense or in truth, Christ is proclaimed."

Let's begin by studying the motives of those who are, indeed, preaching the gospel out of "love" and "good will." These, as Barclay explains, understand that it does not matter who receives the credit, so long as Christ is preached, so long as the gospel expands, and so long as the message of salvation is brought forth to every nation. As Paul writes in 1 Corinthians, these understand that "If I speak with tongues of men and of angels, but do not have love, I have become a noisy gong or a clanging cymbal" (1 Corinthians 13:1). Their love so overarches everything they preach that the words become embodied, "enfleshed," if you will, with purpose. The words of the gospel are not empty and meaningless, but fully formed, and fully informed, by the love they extend. Barclay writes, "when they saw him lying in prison, they redoubled their efforts to preach, and to spread the gospel, so that the gospel would lose nothing because of Paul's imprisonment" (Barclay 1959, 28).

Meanwhile, those preaching the gospel out of "envy," "strife," and "selfish ambition" do so for very different reasons. The Greek word for selfish ambition is *eritheia* (BLB 2016, Strong's G2052), a political term denoting partisanship and fractiousness. It is used to describe one who takes advantage of political expediency to promote themselves. How, then, could Paul permit such men to continue?

It is interesting to set these verses against those in Galatians, which offer a clear rebuke on wrong teaching.

> I am amazed that you are so quickly deserting Him who called you by the grace of Christ, for a different gospel; which is really not another; only there are some who are disturbing you and want to distort the gospel of Christ. But even if we, or an angel from heaven, should preach to you a gospel contrary to what we have preached to you, he

is to be accursed! As we have said before, so I say again now, if any man is preaching to you a gospel contrary to what you received, he is to be accursed! (Galatians 1:6-9)

It is clear that Paul had absolutely no difficulty in providing a scathing rebuke to those who pretended to preach the gospel, so why does he not do so here? The answer, it seems, lies in the motives of those preaching. We've already established that they are less than respectable, being envious and filled with strife and selfish ambition. Guzik writes, "Those who preached Christ for the wrong motive supposed to *add affliction* to Paul's *chains* [NKJV]. Their competitive hearts didn't only want to win for themselves; they also wanted Paul to lose. They wanted Paul to endure the humiliation of having to admit that others were more effective to him" (Guzik 2006a). These men who were preaching from such wrong motives were concerned, like Simon the Magician, not only for their own ambition, but also for the perceived lack in Paul's reputation, which could only serve to further enhance their own.

It is Barclay who suggests that Paul's response reflects a far higher purpose. "Paul knew nothing of personal jealousy; he knew nothing of personal resentment. So long as Jesus Christ was preached Paul did not care who received the credit and the honor and the prestige." He goes on to warn,

"All too often we resent it because someone else gains a prominence or a credit or a prestige which we do not receive." Barclay suggests a more modern context for these verses.

> The intellectuals have no truck with the evangelicals, and the evangelicals impugn the faith of the intellectuals. Those who believe in the evangelism of education have no use for the evangelism of decision, and those who practice the evangelism of decision have no use for those who feel that some other approach will have more lasting effects. (Barclay 1959, 29)

Finally, he emphasizes, "[Paul] was cleansed of self; he had lifted the matter beyond all personalities; all that mattered was that Christ was preached" (Barclay 1959, 29).

In better understanding this concept, I'm reminded of a recent event in a local church in which the Lead Pastor had created such a cult of self around his preaching that when his own indiscretions began to see public light, the entire multi-church system crumbled. Those who attended his congregation were legitimate believers; they loved, and love, Christ. They were led to salvation through the doors of those buildings in which this Pastor preached. Yet, his motives were ultimately shown to be selfish. Does this negate the belief of those who came to know Christ under his tutelage? I think Paul reminds us that the answer is a resounding, "No!"

Certainly, there are those who have turned away, who have been cast into darkness as the cult of self that this Pastor created disintegrated, as his pedestal collapsed; that is an attack of the enemy who takes advantage of our moments of weakness. Yet, many more have gone forth, like a modern diaspora, joining other churches and denominations, and serving God by doing so.

Thus, Paul's words are proven true. "Only that in every way…Christ is proclaimed; and in this I rejoice."

To Live Is Christ and To Die Is Gain

Is it any wonder, having concluded that the highest priority is the preaching of the gospel, that Paul launches into a theological exhortation with some of the strongest language found anywhere in his writing? Indeed, as we look into the next few verses, keep in mind the impact of the words he very deliberately chooses, by the Holy Spirit, to uplift and encourage, to press on and press into Christ Jesus. He begins by repeating, "Yes, and I will rejoice." Not once, that Christ is preached, but twice. Again and again, he returns to this exclamation: *I rejoice, because I am in Christ, because you are in Christ, because we are in Christ, and because Christ is in us!* Before continuing, reread the remainder of Philippians 1, verses 18-26.

Philippians 1:18b-20

Ancient Roman beliefs on such philosophical topics as life and death were complex, but most commentators agree that their interpretation was generally fairly unfavorable. Volatile gods and goddesses lived with human-like foibles: jealousy, spite, anger, and bitterness, committing adultery, waging war, and using individuals as little more than chess pieces in vast and epic inter-personal battles. Political and military coups were common, toppling local and national governments with a regularity that left the general populace reeling. After death, the spirits of those who had passed journeyed to the underworld where the majority could look forward to a passive eternal existence in Asphodel or a torturous penance in Tartarus until they had redeemed themselves. The equivalent of Heaven, the Elysian Fields, were restricted for only the bravest of warriors or the most virtuous of citizens.

With this in mind, read these verses again, noting their strength and power: "earnest expectation," "hope," "boldness," "exalted," and, finally, "life and death." Now, place these declarations of God's glory, grace, and provision against the prevailing Roman culture.

> Ancient Roman attitudes toward life and death were bleak. Death was the inevitable end of life, and suffering in life was just a prelude to that grim fate. Capricious and cruel

> gods exacted inconsistent divine 'justice' with impunity. Humans had no option other than to simply accept the ultimate futility of their aspirations and wishes.
>
> In writing his letter from a place of exceptional suffering, Paul actually reflects that cultural background…with one crucial difference: he offers *joy* from that place. He writes to the Philippians to show them that his imprisonment had not impeded the spread of the gospel, but had actually hastened its expansion. Paul draws attention to the significance of suffering in the growth of God's kingdom, and offers the Philippians that same joy-in-spite-of-suffering if they will embrace that gospel message. (Hall 2016)

This explanation will be important as we continue to study Philippians 1, as the next few verses will expand on Paul's Thesis of Joy. However, in the meantime, I'd like to draw your attention to one final point herein. Take note of the juxtaposition Paul expresses between his prayer for deliverance and the provision of Jesus Christ and his acceptance of the possibility of death on Christ's behalf. While Paul could not have known the future implication of his writing, it is likely that he was well aware of the sweeping martyrdom of Christians across the Roman empire, one that he had participated in, himself, prior to his conversion, and one which had already claimed a number of apostles and disciples. These words were meant to give courage to those facing persecution, following as they are on the previous verses, which expressed his acceptance of his imprisonment in Rome. However, he must have been mindful of the possibility that he, himself, might fall prey to the same fate as so many other early Christians. That he ultimately did only serves to lend further significance to his declarations here and following.

Philippians 1:21-26

Return again to Hall's statement regarding the utter subversion that Paul describes with his Thesis of Joy. Rather than living in apathy and dying in dread, Paul preaches a life where he literally cannot decide whether it is better to die and be with Christ or remain and continue to preach. For an audience of Romans, this was lunacy!

It is, perhaps, difficult to engender a modern understanding of the context I've presented here, engulfed as we are in American commercialism and wealth. Even the poorest among us are in the top 5% of the entire world's income. Nevertheless, it would behoove us to consider what life is like for those in other countries where extreme poverty, unemployment, lack of basic medical care, and early death are inevitable.

Earlier, I described a mission trip that my husband and I undertook to Kenya as college students. It was 2005 and the Kibera slums, outside Nairobi, the capital of Kenya, were widely considered to be some of the largest and worst in the world. Acres upon acres of hovels stood shoulder to shoulder while dirt paths filled with garbage and raw sewage were host to dozens of running, screaming children. This was their playground. At home, they could expect to share, at best, a ten-foot by ten-foot "house" (usually made of little more than cardboard, old wooden slats, or corrugated sheet metal) with as many as a dozen others: grandparents, aunts and uncles, parents, and siblings. Food was scarce, and many resorted to daily visits to the local dump to pick over items discarded by those who were wealthier than they were.

I remember standing on the train tracks overlooking this expanse of desolation and, glancing across the way, seeing a high stone wall, topped with barbed wire, embedded broken glass, and iron spikes which prevented ingress from the slums beyond. On the other side of the wall was a sweeping expanse of green lawn, traveling uphill until it met a wide verandah and a mansion. I don't know who owned this grand house or what they thought of the daily view they had of the Kibera Slums, but it was heartbreaking to see, and to wonder, did these people have no heart for what was literally just before their eyes?

Paul's heart cannot be in doubt. To a people daily walking in the Roman culture, to those in poverty and in need, to the widows and the orphans that Jesus so deeply cared for, Paul preached; and he considered it an honor to remain, preaching for their sake, on par with returning to the loving arms of Christ Jesus and His Heavenly Father. He says, "I do not know which to choose," not "I do not know which is a worse fate," or "I do not know which one I dread more," but the question is which one he ought to reach out and embrace. Ultimately, he chooses to stay, not of his own volition, but because he is wholly at the mercy of Christ and His providential timing. He says, "yet to remain on in the flesh is more necessary for your sake." He remains not for himself, but, hearkening back to his greeting, as a bond-servant of Jesus, called to serve, to preach, to admonish, exhort, and encourage. So, he shall remain a while longer, yet, and he shall do so for their sake. And for our sake as, 2000 years later, we read the words he set to paper on behalf of the Philippians and see their truth ringing across the centuries.

Interestingly, Paul not only decides it is better to remain, but he shares with us a jovial moment, as well, offering a unique wordplay in the following verse that we often miss in most English translations. In Philippians 1:25, he says, "Convinced of this, I know that I will remain and continue with you all for your progress and joy in the faith." An alternative translation here might be that he will "bide and abide," which at least suggests an alliterative, rhyming sense to the words. In truth, the original Greek reads as *menō* and *paramenō*. Barclay offers us a better understanding of these words, though he uses a different Greek rendering.

> The point is this; *menein* simply means *to remain with*; but *paramenein* (*para* is the Greek for *beside*) means to wait beside a person to be ready to help and to help all the time; *paramenein* means not only to *wait*, but to wait ever ready, ever willing and ever able to help. (Barclay 1959, 35)

It is with rich intent that Paul uses these two terms side by side, so whether we understand it best as "remain and continue," or as "bide and abide," or as "remain with and wait, ever ready," it is clear that Paul's intent is not only to remain on earth a while longer, but to remain for the express purpose of further building the Philippians' faith, and ours.

Philippians 1:27-30

As a citizen of Rome by birth, Paul was well acquainted with both the privileges and responsibilities that come with such a station. Likewise, given the population of Philippi and the first converts leading the church there, they, too, would have understood the prerogatives that came with Roman citizenship, but also the burden.

Citizenship is something that many of us take for granted, living in a place and time with nearly unparalleled wealth and prestige, and under-valued for its bestowment at birth. But ask any immigrant, or, more so, any undocumented worker or illegal immigrant, and the idea of citizenship returns to the high ideals that even the most rigid of American forefathers would recognize. In a country where just less than two-thirds of eligible voters actually cast a ballot in the 2012 Presidential Election (File 2013), our understanding of civic responsibility seems deeply flawed.

For many like Paul, however, their Roman citizenship was a prize above nearly any other. Conferred at birth, bought at a heavy price, or earned through upwards of 20 years of military service, Roman citizenship was highly coveted. Paul's own citizenship was granted to him at birth, having been born a freeman in a Roman Free City, Tarsus. What rights and responsibilities, then, did this important legal status grant?

Roman citizens had access to a number of privileges that neither foreigners nor non-citizens could claim. Among the most important were the *suffragium*, the right to vote, including the right to hold a variety of public offices; the *commercium*, the right to draw up contracts, which also included the legal rights to sue (and be sued); and the *conubium*, the right to contract a legal marriage, of which any child would also hold the rights of citizenship (Jahnige 2002). In addition to these, there was the fact that a Roman citizen had the right to a trial, even the right to appeal as high as the emperor, himself, and could not be punished without such legal proceedings (which was the basis for Paul's release and the fear of those who had imprisoned him during his trip to Philippi). Perhaps most importantly, a Roman citizen could not be sentenced to death without first being convicted of treason (the only crime punishable by death) and, even then, would not be required to suffer crucifixion. Christian tradition tells us that it is because of this very law that Nero had Paul beheaded.

In return, however, Roman citizens were required to pay a number of taxes, could be conscripted to the military, and they were required to obey a number of laws, which were codified around 450 BCE and called *The Twelve Tables* (Johnson, Coleman-Norton and Bourne 1961).

It is with this richer understanding of Roman citizenship that Paul proceeds to draw a parallel to our spiritual citizenship in heaven, saying, "Only conduct yourselves in a manner worthy of the gospel of Christ." Like the Romans, Citizens of Heaven have certain rights and responsibilities, as well. As adopted sons and daughters, we are co-inheritors in Christ, saved by Jesus and made clean of our sins by God's divine hand. Paul expands on this explanation in Ephesians.

But God, being rich in mercy, because of His great love with which He loved us, even when we were dead in our transgressions, made us alive together with Christ (by grace you have been saved), and raised us up with Him, and seated us with Him in the heavenly places in Christ Jesus, so that in the ages to come He might show the surpassing riches of His grace in kindness toward us in Christ Jesus. For by grace you have been saved through faith; and that not of yourselves, it is the gift of God; not as a result of works, so that no one may boast. For we are His workmanship, created in Christ Jesus for good works, which God prepared beforehand so that we would walk in them. (Ephesians 2:4-10)

Indeed, a more concise description of not only our rights as Citizens of Heaven, but also our responsibilities, could not be offered. We are saved by grace through faith, not of ourselves or our own actions, but we are, in response, to do good work for His glory. James, too, returns to this theme, saying, "What use is it, my brethren, if someone says he has faith but no works? Can that faith save him?" (James 2:14). The question of works versus faith is far too great to tackle here, but I think at the heart of both James' and Paul's words is the fact that we cannot simply rest on our laurels after having received our citizenship. We must then act upon it, live up to those things that are expected of us at its bestowment, and act in a way that produces good fruit for the kingdom.

Having understood all of this, Paul's next words have all the more impact as he goes on to outline what, exactly, this ought to look like: standing firm in one spirit and in one mind (which is an interesting word play that we will return to when we study Philippians 2), preaching the gospel, and doing so regardless of Paul's presence or absence. UCLA Head Coach John Wooden is quoted as saying, "The true test of a man's character is what he does when no one is watching." I think Paul would agree. In essence, he is telling the Philippians, and, by extension, us: *Your lives ought to enhance God's reputation on earth*. Or, in more common church parlance, *You may be the only Jesus someone ever sees*.

Paul continues, then, to exhort and encourage his dear friends, contrasting the "destruction" of he who would alarm, or affright, the true believer and the "salvation" of that believer when they remain firm in their faith. *Apōleia*, the word used for "destruction," has a number of meanings, including *perdition*, *damnation*, and *death* (BLB 2016, Strong's G684). Meanwhile, *sōtēria*, the word used for "salvation," can be translated as *saved*, *delivered*, or, simply, *health* (BLB 2016, Strong's G4991). In the end, however, he assures them that both are from God and for their own sake. Whether the punishment of the enemy or the exaltation of the Christian, God has both in His hand.

This is how he ends the first chapter of Philippians: not only are both the persecutor and the persecuted within God's hand, but so, too, is the very act of the persecution that they will face for having believed. Paul closes by saying, "For to you it has been granted for Christ's sake, not only to believe in Him, but also to suffer for His sake" (Philippians 1:29). Again, notice his very deliberate word usage, as before, when he spoke of not knowing which to choose, life or death. Paul is reiterating that any suffering, if it is for Jesus' sake, is no hardship at all, but a blessing. *For to you it has been granted...* If we are Citizens of Heaven, then to us it has been given to both glory in our belief, but also to suffer for our faith, as Paul, himself, has suffered in his Roman imprisonment but is established all the more to preach the gospel of Christ Jesus. He invites us, having seen his persecution in Philippi in Acts 16, and now hearing of his further persecution in Rome, to join him, the conflict not being whether or not to believe, but this: "For to me, to live is Christ and to die is gain."

Let us, then, live or die, whichever God has for us, in His Name.

Make My Joy Complete

If Paul used Philippians 1 to set the stage for his major themes – the advancement of the gospel, the participation of the Philippian Church in the ministry, and the unity and community of believers – then Philippians 2 is where he begins to delve more deeply into these theological principles. He discusses the advancement of the gospel through the life of Jesus and the model He provides; the participation of the Philippians in his own ministry and their shared joy in one another; and he not only encourages a continuation of the communal nature of the early church, but also commits two fellow workers into their fold. With all of this in mind, please reread the final verses of Philippians 1, verses 27-30, then continue on to Philippians 2. Remember, our modern translations, which include chapters, paragraphs, and verses, are structured in a manner that is foreign to the original text of Paul's letters, which ought to be read as a whole, transitioning seamlessly from one topic to the next. Once you have done so, please return, again, as we begin our study of Philippians 2.

Philippians 2:1-4

Paul is not mincing words as he launches straight from the previous verses exhorting the Philippians to stand firm in the face of persecution, for they are Citizens of Heaven, to these verses, where he begins to outline what such citizenship ought to entail. In fact, Paul makes it clear that the closing verses of Philippians 1 and the opening verses of Philippians 2 are meant to be connected, one thought flowing to the next, by his use of "therefore." Meaning *consequently* or *because of that*, this word denotes a firm relationship between the previous verses and those which are forthcoming. In essence, this could be read as, *Because you are citizens of heaven, you ought to act in the following manner.* As you study the Bible, be on the lookout for words such as this one, which remind us that verses are not always meant to stand alone but are often better understood within a larger context. What a reflection this is, too, of how the Christian Church ought to function, not standing alone, focused on the individual, but within the larger community of believers, striving together for the sake of the gospel.

Of course, this theme will permeate the entirety of the early part of this chapter, so as we continue, make sure you are taking note of all the different ways in which Paul espouses the importance of Christian community.

In the meantime, however, let us turn our attention to some of the most important aspects of the verses we are studying here. It is always interesting to consider different translations of the same text, gleaning new meaning and connotation as different words and phrases are used. It is for this very reason that a dear friend of mine reads the entire Bible every year (bless her!), each time using a different version. The King James Bible, though not always the most accurate, offers a unique understanding of Philippians 2:1. It reads, "If there be therefore any consolation in Christ, if any comfort in love, if any fellowship of the spirit…" (Philippians 1:1, KJV).

In Luke, we see this same usage as Simeon waits on the arrival of the Messiah. "And there was a man in Jerusalem whose name was Simeon; and this man was righteous and devout, looking for the consolation of Israel; and the Holy Spirit was upon him" (Luke 2:25). While Paul may be known as the Apostle to the Gentiles, he never forgot his inherent Jewishness, and his writing literally drips with Old Testament references and Jewish culture. Further, the idea of "comfort in love" references Paul's earlier letter to the Corinthians, where he writes, "Praise be to the God and Father of our Lord Jesus Christ, the Father of compassion and the God of all comfort" (2 Corinthians 1:3).

The "fellowship of the spirit" is a theme Paul has already presented in Philippians 1:2, wishing the Philippians grace and peace: graciousness and peacefulness among themselves. He further developed it as he shared all of the ways that the Philippians have been participants in the gospel alongside himself. He continues in this chapter, and throughout the remainder of Philippians, to support this thesis. For now, let's peek ahead a few verses, where he says, "But even if I am being poured out as a drink offering upon the sacrifice and service of your faith, I rejoice and share my joy with you all. You too, I urge you, rejoice in the same way and share your joy with me" (Philippians 2:17-18). Paul sees friendship, reciprocity, and sharing as inherent and critical to the idea of Christian fellowship.

In reading these first few verses, then, we can identify several causes of disunity, as well as a number of cures. Paul presents them conversely, though, focusing first, as we ought to as well, on how the Philippians should be acting, then presenting those things which might challenge or divide. Unity ought to be borne out by 1. the encouragement of Christ, 2. the consolation of love, 3. the fellowship of the spirit, 4. affection, and 5. compassion, or mercy, depending on your translation.

On the other hand, the causes of disunity are selfishness, empty conceit, and personal interest. These are interesting words to study, because their roots and connotations are richly nuanced. In fact, one of these words, selfishness, we've seen before! *Eritheia* (BLB 2016, Strong's G2052) is the same word we looked at earlier, when Paul was discussing those who preach the gospel out of "selfish ambition." Recall, if you will, it's political fractiousness, then set is against "regard," which appears later in this verse, also a political term, but one which connotes how one ought to be thinking of a leader or chief, someone with command and authority. Instead of being self-centered, selfish, and divisive, we ought to be lifting others up, as we lift up those in authority over us.

Guzik puts it this way, "If I consider you above me and you consider me above you, then a marvelous thing happens: we have a community where everyone is looked up to, and no one is looked down on" (Guzik 2006b). Barclay explains, "It is when people are really in earnest, when their beliefs really matter to them, when they are eager to carry out their own schemes, that they are apt to get up against each other. The greater their enthusiasm, the greater the danger that they may collide" (Barclay 1959, 40). Barclay's perspective is fascinating in that it entails not only those who are deliberately attempting to subvert the gospel for their own glory, as we saw in Philippians 1:17, but also those who are doing so all unknowingly, out of the best of intentions, but without the cause of love that Paul so deeply espouses to temper their natural enthusiasm.

I've met Christians like this: those who do not understand how deeply they hurt and alienate others through their passion and fervor. Is the gospel innately off-putting and alienating to those without ears to hear? Certainly. Nevertheless, among believers, perhaps the first goal of a Christian ought to be to maintain encouragement, love, fellowship, compassion, affection, and mercy, lest we become like a resounding gong or clanging symbol. I have a toddler at home who likes to bang, bash, crash, and batter. It is difficult to maintain peace amidst such clamor.

Before we continue, there is one more point I'd like to draw our attention to. As an author, I can't help but be impressed by the wordsmithing of a true master, and Paul shows this mastery in Philippians 2:2. Below, I've rendered it in the original Greek, transliterated (a word for word translation without any contextual formatting), and in the finalized NASB version. Note the repetition of word usage in the Greek translation, reflected in the transliteration, and the unfortunate degradation of that word repetition in our finalized version.

Greek:
Plēroō egō chara plēroō hina autos phroneō echō autos agapē sympsychos sympsychos phroneō heis phroneō

Transliteration:
Make my joy complete by [the] same mind, maintaining [the] same love, united in unity, purposed on one purpose.

NASB:
Make my joy complete by being of the same mind, maintaining the same love, united in spirit, intent on one purpose.

I can't help but see this and wonder if Paul is deliberately making a thematic play on words, choosing only those that would repeat, creating a visual image of unity and fellowship even as the words, themselves, express the same!

Philippians 2:5-11

Of this passage Barclay writes, "It would be true to say that in many ways this is the greatest and the most moving passage that Paul ever wrote about Jesus" (Barclay 1959, 42). In its introduction to Philippians, the *NIV Study Bible* says, "[It is] one of the most profound Christological passages in the [New Testament]" (Zondervan 2014). What strikes me most about this passage is that it is the entire gospel message in three sentences. Remember, the Gospels had not yet been written at the time that Paul was writing to

Philippi, so this passage would have embodied the core of early Christian beliefs, and in such a manner as to make it clear, concise, and accessible to the majority of the population to which it was being preached.

Commentators have studied this passage at length, and each one offers up a different perspective. Barclay says of it, "[Paul's] final and unanswerable appeal for unity is to point at the example of Jesus Christ" (Barclay 1959, 43), effectively linking it back to the previous verses. The *NIV Study Bible* states, "Yet, profound as it is, Paul includes it mainly for illustrative purposes" (Zondervan 2014).

I think part of the profoundness of this passage, however, is not necessarily what Paul wrote, though that is critical as well, but what it is that he describes. Namely, he is illustrating the absolute, unchangeable essence of Christ, wholly deified in the very person of God, but also unquestionably and irrefutably man. Yet, even this is not so much a statement as a description of that which was a profound, perhaps even unknowable, miracle of God. Jesus was God. He did not need to "grasp" equality with God because, as most commentators note, he already had it. Yet, for our sake, Jesus left his heavenly throne, put aside that essence, or nature, which was wholly His, and became a man. In *The Jesus I Never Knew*, Philip Yancey describes the circumstances of Jesus' birth. Not only emptied of His deity,

Yancey points to the gospel story of His conception as even further humility.

> Nine months of awkward explanations, the lingering scent of scandal—it seems that God arranged the most humiliating circumstances possible for his entrance, as if to avoid any charge of favoritism. I am impressed that when the Son of God became a human being he played by the rules, harsh rules: small towns do not treat kindly young boys who grow up with questionable paternity. (Yancey 1995, 32-33)

This, too, is a profound statement of Jesus' humanity.

What, then, does Paul expect the Philippians, and us, to make of these statements? He begins, "Have this attitude in yourselves which was also in Christ Jesus," then describes the very being of God becoming a man. How does this in any way relate to a common person, who is neither God nor God incarnate? Returning to our earlier commentary, which suggests this passage is meant to be illustrative, I believe we can find an answer by asking, "What does it intend to illustrate?" In a word, the answer is the humility of Christ. Paul says, "He humbled Himself." If Jesus Christ, the son of God, a part of the triune Deity, could humble himself to become a man, and if, not only that, he could also be "obedient to the point of death, even death on a cross," what excuse have we for acting any differently? Remember, Paul preceded this passage with a discussion of selfishness, empty conceit, and personal interest. Now, with Christ's example, he calls us to a better way, one that involves emptying ourselves, even as Christ did, and becoming obedient, even as Christ did.

To what end? While they had not yet been written, it is hard to miss the gospel parallel when Paul uses such words as "humbled" and "exalted." "But the greatest among you shall be your servant. Whoever exalts himself shall be humbled; and whoever humbles himself shall be exalted" (Matthew 23:11-12). This, Jesus promised the crowds and His disciples, even as he rebuked the Pharisees as hypocrites. Jesus is, Himself, the perfect example of utter humility, from the washing of his disciples' feet to his obedience to death on the cross. If we would wish, then, to follow Him, we, too, must humble ourselves, both before God and before man.

We seem a people today wholly and inordinately consumed by others' perception of us. From the clothes we wear, to the cars we drive, to the homes we buy, to the schools we send our children to, we are like the rich young ruler, who, upon asking Jesus what he must do to enter heaven, "went away grieving" when he was asked to give up his earthly possessions. "It is easier," Jesus goes on to explain, "for a camel to go through the eye of a needle, than for a rich man to enter the kingdom of heaven" (Matthew 19:22, 24).

How are such a people as we are able, then, to humble ourselves to Christ?

Now, don't misunderstand this passage, for when the disciples questioned Jesus as to who, then, could be admitted to heaven, Jesus responded, "With people this is impossible, but with God all things are possible" (Matthew 19:26). Again, a most profound statement: Jesus is saying that, on their own, no one is capable of entering heaven – rich, poor, or otherwise – but through God, any may do so. And yet, it is only by humbling ourselves before God that He is able to make a path for us. What a complex, complicated, yet delightfully simple concept. Simple; not easy.

Fortunately, He makes us this promise: "Take My yoke upon you and learn from Me, for I am gentle and humble in heart, and you will find rest for your souls. For My yoke is easy and My burden is light" (Matthew 11:29-30). Hallelujah!

Paul ends his sweeping Christological passage by describing the exaltation of Christ, that which was promised after His humiliation in Matthew 23:12. Not merely lifted up, resurrected, returned to His prior glory, but given "the name which is above every name, so that at the name of Jesus every knee will bow…and every tongue confess that Jesus Christ is Lord" (Philippians 2:9, 10, 11). What exaltation, indeed! So great was it, in fact, that the earliest Christian creed was simply, "Jesus Christ is Lord!" Barclay says of this kind of worship,

> When men worship Jesus Christ, they do not fall at his feet in broken submission, but in wondering love... It is not the might of Christ which reduces a man to defeated surrender; it is the amazing love of Christ which makes him kneel before Christ in wondering love. Worship is founded, not on fear, but on love. (Barclay 1959, 46-47)

Work Out Your Salvation

A master theologian as well as gifted speaker and missionary, Paul's letters are often saturated with deep spiritual truths too complex for even some seasoned Christians to fully encompass without significant effort. While Philippians, in general, tends more towards the form of an intimate letter between friends, Paul does not shrink from the opportunity to press in closer to the Lord, given the chance. Nor should we. As we prepare for the next section, please return to your Bible and read Philippians 2:12-18.

Philippians 2:12-13

Before we dig into the feast that Paul has laid for us, let's remember some of our previous points of study that warrant repetition in light of these verses because, as we know, this letter is a whole, not merely the product of its various verses, and each thought stems from one previous.

In Philippians 1, Paul told the young church, "Only conduct yourselves in a manner worthy of the gospel of Christ, so that whether I come and see you or remain absent, I will hear that you are standing firm…" (Philippians 1:27). Just a half chapter later, again Paul reminds the young church of their responsibility to do so, but this time, with even further encouragement – not simply exhortation, but commendation for the fact that they have already done so, and then some! "Just as you have always obeyed, not as in my presence only, but now much more in my absence…" (Philippians 2:12). The integrity of the Philippians' belief is beyond question, both in their conduct and their obedience. Paul has no censure to offer them.

Interestingly, it is this same earlier verse, these same words, that first introduce the concept of working out one's faith, as Paul reminds his readers to "conduct" themselves, or act in a manner befitting their position as Citizens of Heaven. Remember that as we studied it, we looked also to James, who reminded us, "What use is it, my brethren, if someone says he has faith but no works? Can that faith save him?" (James 2:14). Again, there is not space here to fully encompass the entire discussion around works versus faith, but I think that if we are willing to dig a bit, we might find an even deeper truth that might suffice to answer both sides of the spectrum.

After commending the Philippians' obedience and integrity, Paul goes on to exhort them to "work out your salvation with fear and trembling" (Philippians 2:12). The Greek word used here is *katergazomai*, which can also be translated as *do*, *perform*, or *cause*. Strong's defines it as "to perform, accomplish, or achieve," "to do that from which something results," "bring about, result in," or to "render one fit for a thing" (BLB 2016, Strong's G2716). It seems clear, then, that the idea of salvation and work are very clearly linked. More than that, they are not only correlated, they appear to be causative. But which ought to engender which? Should salvation result in works, or should works result in salvation?

There are a number of other usages of this word, *katergazomai*, by Paul throughout the New Testament; but instead of chasing down each of those, I'd like to turn, instead, to the idea of work, or labor, being practiced, or "worked out." Proverbs tells us, "The wages of the righteous is life: the income of the wicked punishment" (Proverbs 10:16). An alternative translation of this word, "wages," however, is "work." So then, "The work of the righteous brings life.". Later, in John, we read, "Do not work for the food which perishes, but for the food which endures to eternal life" (John 6:27). 1 Corinthians tells us, "Therefore, my beloved brethren, be steadfast, immovable, always abounding in the work of the Lord, knowing that your toil is not in vain in the Lord" (1 Corinthians 15:58). Finally, in 1 Thessalonians, Paul remembers them in his prayers, "constantly bearing in mind your work of faith and labor of love and steadfastness of hope in our Lord Jesus Christ" (1 Thessalonians 1:3). It seems obvious, then, that work ought to be an integral part to those who are considered Citizens of Heaven, and, more so, should produce fruit. Whether faith begets work, or vice versa, they ought always to be working in tandem for the glory of the kingdom.

The genius of Paul, however, is that having established this relationship, he then proceeds to completely subvert it. In the very next verse, he proclaims, "for it is God who is at work in you" (Philippians 2:13). It is with intent, now, that Paul hearkens back to his earlier words, "For I am confident of this very thing, that He who began a good work in you will perfect it until the day of Christ Jesus" (Philippians 1:6). Indeed, these three verses together, Philippians 1:6, 2:12, and 2:13, seem to suggest a cycle for the in-working of the Holy Spirit in each of us. It is God who begins the work, we who are then called to work it out, yet it is still God who is at work in us. One commentary suggests the following understanding of these verses, "'Salvation' is 'worked in' believers by the Spirit, who enables them through faith to be justified once for all; but it needs to be a progressive work, to be 'worked out' by obedience, through the help of the same Spirit, unto perfection" (Jamieson, Fausset and Brown 1882).

This shifting idea of work, and who is doing it, is further borne out in a translational shift, as well. Though many of our English versions use the same word, "work," in both verses, *katergazomai* in verse 12 becomes *energeō* in verse 13. It is really a disservice to our understanding of these phrases that we lack a similarly nuanced pair of words, because *energeō* means something very different than *katergazomai*. While the latter, as we know, has more to do with the producing of results, the former, according to Strong's means, "To be operative, be at work, put forth power," and "to effect" (BLB 2016, Strong's G1754). In fact, nearly every usage of *energeō* in the New Testament refers to God as being the one who is doing the work, and, interestingly, if not Him, then the enemy. In either case, the effect is always the same: it is another, supernatural force acting upon the person, producing the work in question.

Having then firmly established our understanding of Paul's words here and the remarkable miracle of both the in-working of the Holy Spirit through our salvation and the out-working of our belief through God, we can continue on to the two very critical words Paul uses to describe the work: "fear" and "trembling." These two words are fascinating in both their literal meanings and their symbolic meanings; that is, the allusions they make to the Old Testament.

Beginning with their literal meanings, we see that "fear" is the Greek word *phobos*, which can also be translated as *dread* or *terror* (BLB 2016, Strong's G5401). "Trembling," meanwhile, is the Greek word *tromos*, which means, "quaking in fear" (BLB 2016, Strong's G5156). Both of these meanings depict an air of one who is in terror for his life, quivering in overwhelming and abject horror. This is not, I believe, the message that Paul intended to send. Fortunately, most commentators agree. *Easton's Bible Dictionary* offers this perspective, "[The fear of the Lord] is in the Old Testament used as a designation of true piety. It is a fear conjoined with love and hope, and is therefore not a slavish dread, but rather filial reverence" (Easton 1897a). *Filial reverence.* Given Paul's close, intimate relationship with the Philippians, I can't think of a better phrase to describe the kind of fear he means here.

Hebrews says, may we "offer to God an acceptable service with reverence and awe" (Hebrews 12:28). At the risk of crossing our translations, it is interesting to note that the NLT uses "awe" in place of "fear" in Philippians 2:12, attaining, in essence, the same end as we see here, in Hebrews. The use of the paired words "fear and trembling" also occurs in a number of other places. 2 Corinthians 7:15 and Ephesians 6:5 both use it to describe a posture of humility before one in authority, and Psalms 55:5 and Hebrew 12:21 use equivalent terms.

Interestingly, Strong's also offers an alternative definition for *tromos*. "Used to describe the anxiety of one who distrusts his ability completely to meet all requirements, but religiously does his utmost to fulfil his duty" (BLB 2016, Strong's G5156). In light of our complex discussion regarding both the in-working of the Spirit and the out-working of God in us, this seems an especially apt translation. The calling of God is often so great that it would be impossible to accomplish without His hand; yet, as we walk out our faith, day by day, He equips us for success. This translation, then, places us in a position of humility, recognizing our own lack, but, by faith, allowing God to accomplish His work in us. Paul is able to link both concepts, then: to work out our salvation and the posture in which we ought to be doing it.

Before moving on, I want to present one more commentary on this theme of fear of the Lord because I believe it makes a compelling case both for our own posture of humility before the authority of God, and also because it echoes Barclay's earlier words on the topic of fear. Remember, we closed our last chapter with his words, "Worship is founded, not on fear, but on love" (Barclay 1959, 47). W. L. Walker offers this explanation,

> Fear is a natural and, in its purpose, beneficent feeling, arising in the presence or anticipation of danger and moving to its avoidance; it is also awakened in the presence of superiors and of striking manifestation of power, taking the form of awe or reverence. Fear has been said to be the source of religion, but religion can never have originated in fear, alone, since men are impelled to draw nigh with expectation to the object of their worship. (Walker 1939)

I have read and studied this passage for months, first for our Women's Bible Study, where it first caught my attention, and now, later, in preparation to write about it here. My awe for it remains, however, unabated! Earlier in my Christian journey, I read the phrase "fear and trembling" and thought to myself, *Indeed, it is a great work God is asking of us. It ought to instill fear! Fear of inadequacy, fear of failure, fear of God, who calls us to greater and higher things than we can imagine.* I am reminded of the old adage among Christians that if God showed us today where we would be in ten, twenty, or thirty years, we might run in fear, and well we should, because how could we ever hope to rise to God's call? Now, though, I read these passages and think of Abraham, who, though he feared to lose everything, including his own son, yet obeyed God, and was so richly blessed for it. I think of Paul, beaten and thrown into a Philippian prison, overcoming his fear with praise and worship, and the invitation that gave God place to move mightily in the heart of the jailer. Today, I see it very differently. Let me stand in awe of the great hand of God, with fear, yes, and also reverence, for His work is mighty, and beyond any ability of mine, yet He calls me, and He blesses me to partake, nonetheless. One translation, in particular, stands out to me, then, as I read these verses. The Aramaic Bible says, "Do the service of your life" (Philippians 2:12, ABPE). What higher calling could there be?

Philippians 2:14-18

As we have already discussed, despite his calling to the Gentiles, Paul never lost even the slightest iota of his inherent Jewishness. He hearkened often to Old Testament beliefs, laws, and traditions that newer, Gentile Christians might not understand, also setting a foundation for future readers – both those coming from the Jewish faith and those who acknowledge the profound power and truth of the Old Testament, even in light of Christ's displacement of much of it.

It is easy to fall into the trap of believing that the Old Testament is nothing more than stories or, at best, dry, boring history. As Christians, we are told that Christ overcame the Law, "by abolishing in His flesh the enmity, which is the Law of commandments contained in ordinances" (Ephesians 2:15). Yet, as Yancey clearly articulates, Jesus, himself, was wholly Jewish, and his entire ministry focused first on those who shared his unique heritage (Yancey 1995). To completely dismiss the Old Testament, then, is to fall prey to one of the enemy's greatest lies. As contemporary Christians with access to both Testaments, multiple versions and translations, and all of the modern Bible study tools at our disposal, even more so, we must not believe that there is nothing for us in the Old Testament.

With this in mind, I'd like to turn for just a moment to Exodus. As a Jew of Jews, you will see, Paul never lost sight of either his heritage or the powerful symbolism it contained. Only three days after witnessing the parting of the Red Sea, after seeing the complete and utter destruction of Pharaoh and his armies, we find the Israelites wandering in the wilderness, and "the people grumbled at Moses, saying, 'What shall we drink?'" (Exodus 15:24). God provides sweet water to them, through the medium of Moses, yet only a few weeks later, again, "The whole congregation of the sons of Israel grumbled against Moses and Aaron in the wilderness" (Exodus 16:2). Water was not enough; now, they required food, and manna was provided. Yet again, only a few weeks later, the miraculous manna isn't enough, either. And on and on it goes. Nothing ever seems to be quite enough to fully sate the empty and barren spirits of those wandering the desert. Finally, God answers, "I have heard the grumblings of the sons of Israel; speak to them, saying, 'At twilight you shall eat meat, and in the morning you shall be filled with bread; and you shall know that I am the Lord your God.'" (Exodus 16:12).

Is it any wonder, then, that as Paul exhorts the Philippians, "do all things without grumbling or disputing," that his command to them carries such a greater weight than a casual reading could bestow? Paul is, in essence, warning the Philippians against the same kind of attitude that so impacted his own forebears, leading, ultimately, to their curse to wander forty years in the desert, denying an entire generation entrance into the promised land. Not only that, but he goes on, encouraging them to be "blameless and innocent…above reproach." Even the most cursory reading of Exodus cannot help but yield example after example of the former, with so very few examples of the latter. Paul reminds the Philippians, and all readers, of the price of disobedience, dissatisfaction, and dissonance.

These words remind his listeners, too, of the very words that Christ spoke to his disciples: "Behold, I send you out as sheep in the midst of wolves; so be shrewd as serpents and innocent as doves…" (Matthew 10:16). However, Paul presses the metaphor further, reminding his readers, again, of the Old Testament. In Deuteronomy, we read, "They have acted corruptly toward Him, they are not His children, because of their defect; but are a perverse and crooked generation" (Deuteronomy 32:5). Paul does not use these same words accidentally; he is issuing a warning to all believers, a clarion call that cannot be ignored, except at the peril of one's soul.

The Greek word for crooked is *skolios*, the word from which we get the medical condition scoliosis. As many of my generation experienced, I have memories of standing in the gym locker room in middle and high school and having my back examined for any sign of scoliosis, though I know at the time I did not understand the implications of such a disease. Years later, while working with the clinic in Kenya, our team was joined by another one, a group of doctors who were performing scoliosis corrections to those suffering from this debilitating malformation. We were able to look at their x-rays and see spines bent nearly double, lungs all but crushed by the very bone structures designed to protect them, heads pulled into the most grotesque of positions, forcing the patient into an eternal attitude of perverted submission.

Afterwards, we met with some of these patients, now straight-backed and in braces, sitting upright for the first time in their lives. We saw more x-rays showing long, steel rods grafted to the bones of their spines. We looked into their eyes and saw hope for the first time; the hope of people who had resigned themselves to a life of debilitating defect and, for the first time, have seen a future beyond it. It was a reflection of our own prosthetics work but magnified by the extent of their previous injury. Tears come to my eyes even now, thinking of what the most minor of medical procedures in the US can produce in a country lacking this basic medical care.

"Perverse," on the other hand, means "to distort, turn aside, to pervert, corrupt" (BLB 2016, Strong's G1294). While "crooked" might give us an idea of an outward form, "perverse" brings us within. I'll return to this idea a little later, but for now, I hope that both Paul's literal and symbolic meanings are clear to you. Like the Israelites in the desert, there is so much risk in forgetting the goodness of God, His provision, and His glory. Fortunately, Paul offers an alternative, one that he is, of course, confident the Philippians have already embraced. They are to stand firm in the midst of such ugly men, "among whom you appear as lights in the world." His word for "lights" is *phōstēr*, which can mean "of the stars, sun and moon" (BLB 2016, Strong's G5458). For "world," he uses *kosmos* (BLB 2016, Strong's G2889), which, of course, is where our modern word *cosmos* to describe the universe comes from. Not just lights in the world, then, but shining like stars, like the sun, even, in the dark expanse of the universe!

Paul finishes these verses with an athletic picture. Barclay writes,

> In every Greek city the gymnasium was far more than a physical training-ground. It was in the gymnasium that Socrates so often talked…it was in the gymnasium that the philosophers and the sophists and the wandering teachers and preachers so often found their audience. In any Greek city, the gymnasium was not only the physical training-ground, it was also the intellectual club of the city. (Barclay 1959, 56)

Paul so often relied on the visual of an athlete because it was one that would be wholly familiar to his entire Greek and Roman audience. Central to the lifestyle of most of his contemporaries, the idea of "running the race" would have been supremely accessible to those hearing his words. That it would neither be in toil nor in vain, but that it would result in success, further paints this picture, keeping in mind the origin of the Olympic Games in ancient Greece and Rome. Superseding even the most vicious wars, the victors were crowned with wreaths of laurel and presented medals of honor. This is the vision that Paul alludes to here, crowned in glory not by the might of Caesar, but by the High King of Heaven, Himself.

Yet, in reading these words, I can't help but be reminded of the inverse. Sometimes we do, in fact, toil in vain. How disappointing and depressing that can be, too. Have you ever invested deeply in another, invested time, energy, love, attention, and every good thing, as Paul is so clearly doing with his dear friends in Philippi? Imagine if their response was not what we read here, but more akin to that of the Galatians, who had so quickly fallen away, or of Philemon, whose reception to the return of Onesimus, his runaway slave, is unknown to us. What then? Is the work in vain? Paul certainly didn't think so. He says, "even if I am being poured out as a drink offering upon the sacrifice and service of your faith, I rejoice."

    Again, we turn to the Old Testament to better understand this idea of sacrifice, recognizing that drink offerings brought to the tabernacle or the temple were poured over the holy fire, wholly consumed by God, an act of divine worship. Remember Elijah's altar in 1 Kings 18 where, in a test against the priests of Baal, the entirety was doused in water three times, until the wood was drenched and the trench around the altar filled with water like a moat. After Elijah prayed, "the fire of the Lord fell and consumed the burnt offering and the wood and the stones and the dust, and licked up the water" (1 Kings 18:38). When God consumes us, he does so completely, leaving nothing behind, not even the stones of the foundation we have built our lives upon, nor the dust of its construction, nor even the drink offering, itself. Paul calls himself little more than that which is poured out before God, wholly consumed by Him, to His ends, not to Paul's own, or even to his beloved friends at Philippi. And when God does consume us, we are reminded, and brought full circle, as well, it is not our own work, but "it is God who is at work" (Philippians 2:13).

Within and Without

Paul has, up to this point, been playing a subtler game with his words than we have even yet discovered, and it is here that I want to pause and bring our attention to this, because to miss it might be to miss one of the most important aspects of this chapter. This first half of Philippians 2 is rife with symbolic contrast between the inward attitude and the outward behavior. Let's look at a few verses where this is done. As we do so, please note where I have **bolded** an inward attitude and *italicized* an outward behavior.

"Do nothing from *selfishness* or **empty conceit**, but with **humility** of mind *regard one another* as more important than yourselves; do not merely look out for your own **personal interests**, but also for the *interests of others*." (Philippians 2:3-4)

"*Work out* your salvation with fear and trembling; for it is God who is **at work** in you…" (Philippians 2:12-13)

"Do all things without **grumbling** or *disputing*…" (Philippians 2:14)

"So that you will prove yourselves to be *blameless* and **innocent**, children of God above reproach in the midst of a *crooked* and **perverse** generation…" (Philippians 2:15)

"But even if I am being poured out as a drink offering upon the *sacrifice* and **service** of your faith…" (Philippians 2:17)

Over and over, Paul has set these two ideas against each other, the inward attitude and the outward behavior, reminding us that one will always lead to the other. The old adage "garbage in, garbage out" holds so true in our attitudes and faith. If we think on negative things, focus on our disappointments, and find fault in every situation, our outward words and actions will reflect that. But if we focus on our joy, with thanksgiving and praise, as Paul did in the Philippian jail, we are reminded of God's greatness, and our humility and our attitudes will reflect that, as well. Paul ends, however, as he always does, by offering a greater truth:

"Rejoice in the same way and share your joy with me." Inwardly and outwardly, both, let us share together in our mutual joy.

Hold Men Like Him in High Regard

As we enter into our study of this next portion of scripture, I confess, I have struggled to find its place within the larger context of Philippians. Perhaps it lends further credence to Swift's assertion that the central theme of the entire Book of Philippians is that of participation in the gospel. It certainly seems so, especially following so closely on the heels of Paul's exhortation to share their mutual joy with one another. In any case, as we read the next few verses, I'm confident that God has things yet to reveal, and He will do so, if we only ask. So, let us do so praying for revelation and insight once again, then pausing a moment to read Philippians 2:19-30.

Philippians 2:19-24

At first glance, these verses seem quite straightforward. Before we delve more deeply into their meaning, I want to encourage you to simply soak in the genuine affection Paul holds for both Timothy and the church at Philippi. If Paul is looking for the perfect lens through which to illustrate the sharing of joy together, he has found it here: his own joy in Timothy, like a son to him; his joy in the Philippians and his concern for their welfare; and his belief that Timothy's journey will serve to encourage both them and himself in the Lord. Shared joy, indeed.

Beyond this first, obvious layer, however, we see the continuation of a previous discussion. Remember, Paul has called the Philippians to a high level of conduct, the responsibility of their Citizenship in Heaven weighing upon them. He has sent his own encouragement and exhortation, and now hopes to be encouraged, in return. As in 1:27 and 2:12, his faith in their ability to produce is absolute. He does not say, *that I might be encouraged if I hear you are doing well.* Instead, there is little doubt, "so that I also may be encouraged *when* I learn of your condition." As he is firmly convinced the Philippians shall be proved before God, he also believes that he, himself, will be fully justified in his faith in them. In fact, it is interesting to note the many reciprocal relationships Paul has set forth in this letter: between himself and God, between himself and the Philippians, between himself and Timothy, between the Philippians and God, and, in just a moment, between the Philippians and Timothy. If participation, sharing, and fellowship are, indeed, his central theme, it would be hard to miss all of the ways in which he has illustrated it.

In Philippians 1:1, we learned that Paul's greeting to the Church at Philippi was, in part, to establish his authority to teach them, which came from his status as a slave or bond-servant of Christ. However, we did not discuss Timothy's inclusion in the greeting, and with good reason, else we would not have the opportunity to explore it here. So, with that in mind, let's reread the opening verse of Philippians, "Paul and Timothy, bond-servants of Christ Jesus" (Philippians 1:1). Note, if you would, that Paul does not refer to only himself as a bond-servant of Christ, but that it is in the plural, meaning that he sees both himself *and* Timothy in this role. Not only is he establishing his right to teach them, he is establishing Timothy's authority, as well. Of course, Timothy would be as known to the Philippians as Paul, himself, having been part of the party (with Silas) who originally attended Philippi and, some commentators suggest, in acting as a messenger for Paul, may have actually visited them more often than his mentor.

Paul grants his own authority to teach, and that of God, as well, in a number of specific compliments. He calls Timothy a "kindred spirit," "genuinely concerned for [their] welfare." He is of "proven worth," serving Paul, personally, "like a child serving his father." Too, he establishes an inverse relationship, pointing out all those who "seek after their own interests," then setting Timothy in opposition, implying that he seeks first the interests of Jesus Christ. We should all hope to receive such high commendation from those who have mentored us.

I am reminded, again, of Beth Moore's *Mercy Triumphs*, where she attests, "Jesus radically restructures the idea of family" and invites us to "consider what seems to be the progression: Natural Family -> Family + Disciples -> Disciples – Family -> Spiritual Family -> Resurrected Family" (Moore 2011, 13). In her explanation, Moore suggests that Jesus shifted the idea of family through the illustration of his own life, beginning with the record of his birth and childhood among his own family, then pointing us to John 2:12, where he was joined by both his family and his disciples at the wedding in Cana. In Mark 3:31-35, Jesus deliberately moves away from his natural family, rejecting the idea that they ought to be of more import to him than what we would colloquially today call our "brothers and sisters in Christ." Returning to John, verses 19-27, we see the next step in the progression as Jesus calls upon John to care for his own mother, creating an idea of spiritual family that is central to our understanding of spiritual fellowship today. Finally, Jesus returns in Acts 1:12-14, and we see a dramatic reconciliation between Jesus and one of his brothers, James, who would later go on to lead the early Christian church in Jerusalem!

In my own life, I come from a family of non-believers (natural family). I was led to Christ by a dear "sister," whose family "adopted" me, taking responsibility for my early understanding of my faith (family + disciples). Entering college far from home, I was surrounded by other believers, each playing a role in encouraging my own journey and one, ultimately, becoming the man I would marry (disciples – family). Perhaps you could call entering into his family (all believers) my entrance into a "spiritual family" of my own. Finally, I've been blessed with a number of amazing women who have loved and mentored me in a way that allows me to truly call myself a "daughter in Christ." Family has been resurrected for me in this way, even as I continue to love my natural family and hope and believe in their salvation. Yet, to be set apart, to be holy, to be a Citizen of Heaven entails, too, a separation from the things of this world and of the flesh, so we must find our home first amongst those who believe as we do.

I can't help but wonder if Paul experienced a similar progression in his own life. Being raised a Jew, I can't imagine his conversion didn't cause at least a little strain with his family. They are never referred to, as far as we can tell, which probably means that they were not playing a significant role in his life by the time his ministry really began to flourish. Perhaps they were already dead, but if that were the case, we could expect at least some kind of passing reference to their role in his life. Instead, Paul's journey is described by those he fellowshipped with. Later, he experiences his own spiritual family in the form of Timothy, a son committed to him by God. Perhaps he did, in fact, experience Moore's "resurrected family," perhaps not. As is the case even today, sometimes we are blessed to be joined by those we love in our faith, but sometimes we are not so lucky. Perhaps, for Paul, his resurrected family was his firm belief in God the Father, His Son, Jesus Christ, and his calling to love and care for the fledgling Gentile churches, his brothers and sisters in Christ. And that, too, is a precious illustration for those of us who continue to hope and pray but may not experience the salvation of our families for which we long.

In any case, Paul stood firm, here, commending Timothy to the Philippians and sharing his own desire to visit them as soon as possible. Remember, Paul was in Rome awaiting trial, but his hope was in the Lord and his faith was that he would be acquitted and freed – and soon – so that he could then visit his beloved brethren.

Philippians 2:25-27

Having commended Timothy and established his authority before the Philippians, Paul continues, now, by doing the same for Epaphroditus, who was the one responsible for bringing the gift of the Philippians to Paul, and then tasked to remain and serve him in whatever manner he saw fit. Guzik notes three special honors that Paul bestows upon Epaphroditus, "Brother speaks of a relationship to be enjoyed. Worker speaks of a job to be done. Soldier speaks of a battle to be fought... He was a man Paul valued as a partner in the work of ministry" (Guzik 2006b).

While we translate it as "messenger," the word Paul uses here is actually the Greek *apostolos* (BLB 2016, Strong's G652), from which we get the word apostle, a word that "Christian usage had consecrated and ennobled...and by using it Paul, by implication, ranks Epaphroditus with himself and all the apostles of Christ, with the very spiritual elite of the faith" (Barclay 1959, 61). *Smith's Bible Dictionary*, in turn, suggests that "minister" here is more akin to that of a "voluntary attendant on another. In the Old Testament it is applied to an attendance upon a person of high rank" (Smith 1901). In essence, Paul is calling Epaphroditus not only a man of high repute, a fellow worker, soldier, and brother, but also an apostle of Christ Jesus. Barclay writes, "Epaphroditus was one with Paul in sympathy, one with him in work, one with him in danger" (Barclay 1959, 61), a symbolic representation of the very attitude of the Philippians, themselves. His voluntary act of service, a sacrifice in its own right, recalls Paul's previous words just a few verses ago, "even if I am being poured out as a drink offering upon the sacrifice and service of your faith, I rejoice..." (Philippians 2:17). Indeed, Epaphroditus' service and sacrifice nearly cost him his life.

Perhaps it was with Epaphroditus' illness in mind that Paul had earlier written, "For to me, to live is Christ and to die is gain" (Philippians 1:21). Certainly, Epaphroditus came nigh unto walking this verse out, and those following, which hold the promise of "the desire to depart and be with Christ, for that is very much better" (Philippians 1:23). Yet, God had mercy. We do not hear again of Epaphroditus, but we must believe that God's healing served some higher purpose. Whether it was only to spare Paul further grief, whether it was to return and encourage the Philippians, or whether he, himself, went on to serve the faith in some great, yet unrecorded, way, we'll never know. Nevertheless, Paul is grateful, illustrating for us that, though sorrow may inflict itself upon even the most faithful and devoted of Christ-followers, God's goodness, grace, and mercy may yet overcome. It is not in feeling sadness, then, that we are led to disobedience, but in allowing this passing feeling to subvert our faith and give the enemy a foothold for disbelieving God. Paul stands firm, yet it is only by the grace of God and his mercy "not on him only, but also on me," that he does not fall into the trap.

Philippians 2:28-30

Commentators note that Epaphroditus' return to Philippi could easily have been steeped in shame. In fact, recall that which had caused the explosion between Paul and Barnabas in Acts 15:37-39: the perceived lack in Barnabas' nephew, John Mark, who had already abandoned the mission field once before. Sent home, deficient in his service, and embarrassed by Paul's rejection, Epaphroditus, too, might have faced similar rejection had Paul not intervened. While the situations certainly seem to differ, and perhaps because Paul, too, is older and wiser, he shows tremendous empathy for Epaphroditus' position, already commending him, now doing so again.

My husband's grandparents have lived in Germany all their lives, an entire continent and an ocean away from us, and have struggled with ill health for a number of years. His grandmother passed earlier this year; and we just recently received word that his grandfather, too, may be very close to the end. I think I can understand a bit of Epaphroditus' distress, knowing that the Philippians had heard he was ill, and Paul's concern, too, that they see him again and rejoice. Even with modern communication, it is devastating to receive news of each hospitalization and emergency, wondering if this will be the one that heralds the end, trying to decide each time if we should make an unplanned visit, scared that if we wait too long, we won't have the chance, but mindful that we cannot go every time something comes up. How much more so must the Philippians have felt this, in an age when a single message might take weeks to be delivered, and Epaphroditus might already have been long dead by the time they even received news of his illness? In return, how difficult to know that those you love most wait in an agony of dread for word, one way or the other.

How I wish that our Apa could rise from his bed and hasten to us, or us to him, to reassure ourselves that he remains with us just a bit longer. How we worry for the day when that final call comes. How, in between, we wonder and wait, never quite knowing.

I think it is with this in mind that Paul hastens Epaphroditus home again, his love for the small church at Philippi echoing through the centuries, seeking to relieve their distress and concern. Yet, even overwhelmed as he might have been by his own challenges, his impending trial, and his constant thorn, he seeks to smooth Epaphroditus' return. He exhorts, "Receive him then in the Lord with all joy, and hold men like him in high regard." There can be no doubt that his return is not in shame or ignominy, then, but in triumph, having risked his life, literally *gambled* or *hazarded* (Vines 1940b) it on behalf of the Philippians. Like Mother Theresa at her leprosy clinic in India, or those who remained behind when the great nuclear reactor at Fukushima began to melt down, Epaphroditus threw the dice with his very life, and Paul would ensure that his commitment would not be forgotten.

As we end this chapter, I want to touch on a final point, one that I struggled with in my initial readings of Philippians. What was the lack that Paul describes as he commends Epaphroditus? He says, "risking his life to complete what was deficient in your service to me," yet, up to this point, it appears there has been no lack on the part of the Philippians to speak of. It is Guzik who suggests "There was a lack in all the Philippians' generosity and good intentions until the gift finally made its way to Paul's need." He goes on to say, "We should have the heart that there is something lacking in our service until the job is done. We should not be satisfied with good intentions or a half-done job" (Guzik 2006b). The lack, or deficiency, then, was in actually transporting their gift to Paul. It is not enough to have good intentions, or even to begin on a path; we must complete our journey, following through to the very end, in order to find ourselves triumphant. Because of his service, Epaphroditus returns to Philippi wreathed in laurels of victory, not toiling in vain, but rejoicing in the work of Christ.

The Righteousness Which Comes from God

As the year winds down and the holidays loom, I'm struggling to maintain my motivation. A month ago, I thought I could be done writing this book by year's end, even looked forward to finishing early. But life happened, as it so often does. At the end of November, we did, indeed, lose our dear Apa. The toddler got sick. We spent literal days on end on an airplane traveling halfway around the world. Now, I'm discouraged to find that not only will it not be complete, it looks to stretch out well into the new year. So quickly do we, as humans, swing between extremes: joy to discouragement, courage to fear, strength to weakness. In the blink of an eye, all that seemed golden in the light turns tarnished. It is now, then, that Paul's words return to me. "But one thing I do, forgetting what lies behind and reaching forward to what lies ahead, I press on towards the goal for the prize of the upward call of God in Christ Jesus" (Philippians 3:13-14). Let us press on, then, together. Let us answer the call of Christ. Let us lay aside the things that hinder and entangle us (Hebrews 12:1, NIV) and let us run neither in toil nor in vain, but in the glory we have received from Christ Jesus. With all of this in mind, please read Philippians 3:1-9, remembering all that we have already studied, then return here, where we shall, indeed, continue our journey.

Philippians 3:1-3

If Philippians 1 was Paul's thesis statement and Philippians 2 was his supporting arguments, then Philippians 3 could easily be seen as his expected results. Having established the theories, he now shows how they might be executed and, as such, it is hard to miss the many times in this chapter that Paul begins ticking off points on his metaphorical fingers. Indeed, right away we see two of these lists: three things of which the Philippians should be aware and three ways in which they have not fallen prey to that trap.

Beginning with Paul's warnings, we read, "Beware of the dogs, beware of the evil workers, beware of the false circumcision." While all three could easily be read as separate cautions, they are, in fact, one: multi-faceted, but posing a unique hazard to the young church at Philippi. Matthew Henry describes the challenge this way, "It seems the church of the Philippians, though a faithful and flourishing church, was disturbed by the Judaizing teachers, who endeavoured to keep up the law of Moses, and mix the observances of it with the doctrine of Christ and his institutions" (Henry 1706a). Paul's warning, then, is that the Philippians ought to allow such teachers no quarter.

There is much to be made today of the idea of Christ as a subversive or revolutionary. Yancey, in fact, explains how Jesus was born into a hotbed of revolutionary activity in his book *The Jesus I Never Knew*. Paul, too, fits this mold, easily subverting both the religious and political teachings of the day to his own purposes. We see him do it again, here, as he takes the Jewish slur for Gentiles, "dogs," wild, aggressive, noisy, diseased, and turns it on its head. As Jesus so often preached, that those who thought they had much had, in fact, nothing, so Paul, too, suggests as much. The Judaizers, those of the Law who believed the Gentiles were forbidden from heaven by virtue of their lack of circumcision, are now told that they, themselves, shall not be granted admittance.

Continuing, Paul calls them "evil workers." Though we might read this as "those who are working evil," most commentators agree that it would be more correct to interpret it as "those who, through attempting to justify their righteousness through works, are evil." This also more closely aligns this warning with the one preceding, calling them dogs, and the one directly to follow. Paul has already waxed eloquent on his position regarding works versus faith, as we have, as well, though it is worth noting that he will reiterate it once again in a moment.

Finally, Paul speaks of "the false circumcision;" that is, those who have been circumcised in the flesh, but not in the Spirit. Many Jews, including Paul, himself, prior to his conversion, could be found guilty of this charge: so concerned with upholding Mosaic Law that they forgot its spirit, the very heart of God which drove Him to lay forth such precepts. We are in danger of doing the same today, as Christians spend so much time in political turmoil over legalistic interpretations of the Word. We stand in danger of forgetting that first and foremost, overarching all other commands, Jesus told us in Luke, "You shall love the Lord your God with all your heart, and with all your soul, and with all your strength, and with all your mind; and your neighbor as yourself" (Luke 10:27). So important was this command that Matthew, too, recorded it. "And He said to him, 'YOU SHALL LOVE THE LORD YOUR GOD WITH ALL YOUR HEART, AND WITH ALL YOUR SOUL, AND WITH ALL YOUR MIND.' This is the great and foremost commandment. The second is like it, 'YOU SHALL LOVE YOUR NEIGHBOR AS YOURSELF.' On these two commandments depend the whole Law and the Prophets.'" (Matthew 22:37-39). In fact, Matthew's recording is even more emphatic, placing as it does Jesus' command within the context of Old Testament history. It would behoove us, then, to return, once again, to 1 Corinthians, where Paul warns, "If I speak with tongues of men and of angels, but do not have love, I have become a noisy gong or a clanging cymbal" (1 Corinthians 13:1). Without love, we, ourselves, are nothing more than law-ridden, clanging noise.

Yet, by grace, Paul reminds us of another option. Not subsumed by the black and white legalism of the day, he reassures his readers, "we are the true circumcision." Having presented three things of which to beware, Paul now reflects on three ways in which we are proved: "we…who worship in the Spirit of God and glory in Christ Jesus and put no confidence in the flesh." As we discuss the idea of "true circumcision," we might be well-served to be reminded of several times Paul has advocated on behalf of Gentile non-circumcision. In Acts, you will remember, he and Barnabas went before the Council at Jerusalem and spoke of the miracles God had performed among the Gentiles. He remembers this interview in Galatians.

> But on the contrary, seeing that I had been entrusted with the gospel to the uncircumcised, just as Peter had been to the circumcised (for He who effectually worked for Peter in his apostleship to the circumcised effectually worked for me also to the Gentiles), and recognizing the grace that had been given to me, James and Cephas and

> John, who were reputed to be pillars, gave to me and Barnabas the right hand of fellowship, so that we might go to the Gentiles and they to the circumcised. (Galatians 2:7-9)

Before James, Peter, and John, he had already argued his case, and won. Any who preached otherwise served only as stumbling blocks to true believers.

Worshiping in the Spirit of God, then, we are reminded of the tongues of flame descending from heaven and settling on the heads of those gathered on the Day of Pentecost (Acts 2:1-4). As we glory in Christ Jesus, we are reminded that our glory *is* Christ Jesus, alone, and nothing by which we could make any claim to righteousness of ourselves. Finally, as we put no confidence in the flesh, either ourselves or the things of this world, we are forced, therefore, to fix our eyes on heaven and the Holy Trinity: God the Father, Jesus His Son, and the Holy Spirit, all three of which are perfectly bound in Paul's words to the Philippians, and all of which point us back to the opening words of this chapter: "rejoice in the Lord."

Paul calls this repetition *asphalēs* (BLB 2016, Strong's G804), or "a safeguard," but the word is more nuanced than that. Strong's often translates it as either *certain* or *sure*, both of which suggest more than simple safety, but a certainty, or surety, that repetition will lead to absolute belief and knowledge. The more Paul says it, the more they hear it, the more likely they are to fully encompass it, like the Old Testament practice of carving the Law into the door frames and lintels. In doing so, they will have surety against the false teachers that Paul is about to warn them of. As Paul says in Galatians, "But even if we, or an angel from heaven, should preach to you a gospel contrary to what we have preached to you, he is to be accursed! As we have said before, so I say again now, if any man is preaching to you a gospel contrary to what you received, he is to be accursed!" (Galatians 1:8-9). By continuing to confirm his message, Paul safeguards them against any other that might lead them astray, including any forgeries that might have been circulating at the time purporting to be written by him (see 2 Thessalonians 2:2). Charles Spurgeon notes, "Some hearers are like the Athenian academicians; they want to hear something new. The apostle says, 'To have the same things written to you, is safe.' So it is for us; to have the same gospel, the same Jesus, the same Holy Spirit, made known to us, is safe. New doctrine is dangerous doctrine" (Spurgeon, Spurgeon's Sermons Volume 39: 1893 1893).

  Guzik, meanwhile, focusses on that which Paul is repeating, namely, to rejoice in the Lord. He reminds us that it is not in circumstances, or things of the flesh, or in ourselves that we ought to rejoice, but in the Lord, alone, once again pointing us towards Paul's description of those who are of the true circumcision (Guzik 2006c). In fact, Paul's commitment to repetition is clear, making this instance the sixth of nine times he will remind his readers of this precept in this letter (see 1:18, 2:17, 2:18, 2:28, 3:1, 4:4, and 4:10). F. B. Meyer emphasizes, then, on this topic of rejoicing, "It is a duty for us to cultivate this joy. We must steadfastly arrest any tendency to murmur and complain; to find fault with God's dealings; or to seek to elicit sympathy. We must as much resist the temptation to depression and melancholy as we would to any form of sin" (Meyer n.d.).

Philippians 3:4-9

Having reminded the Philippians of the three ways in which they are the "true circumcision," in worshipping in the Spirit of God, in glorying in Christ Jesus, and in putting no confidence in the flesh, Paul continues by presenting himself as the consummate example, both in what he has given up and in what he has gained.

If Jesus was the perfect example of grace on Earth, I think it could be argued that Paul was his counterpart, the perfect example of the Law. Paul was born into it, circumcised the eighth day, of the nation of Israel, of the tribe of Benjamin, a Hebrew of Hebrews. Wuest writes,

> Paul was a citizen of Tarsus. At the time he lived there, only families of wealth and reputation were allowed to retain their Tarsian citizenship. This throws a flood of light upon Paul's early life. He was born into a home of wealth and culture. His family were wealthy Jews living in one of the most progressive of oriental cities. (Wuest 2015)

More applicable to us, though, is the fact that Paul chose the Law. Today's Christians, though sometimes our Christian culture might suggest differently, must do the same. Each of us must choose, intimately and personally, to accept the gift of grace that Jesus offers, to be covered by His blood, to open the door when He knocks. Paul chose the Law as much as he was born to it, describing himself as a Pharisee, a sect of Jewish faith which was well-known for abiding by the minutiae of every aspect of the Law, describing himself as zealous and a persecutor, describing himself as blameless in the Law, utterly righteous in every way. These are quite the claims, as the specificity of the Law which the Pharisees practiced was near impossible to successfully navigate. Spurgeon says, "There is no man who stood so good a chance of being justified by works as Paul did, if there could have been any justification in that way" (Spurgeon 1910).

In short, Paul was the perfect example of a Pharisee and a Jew, righteous and blameless in every way that didn't count.

Yet, when he was faced with Jesus on the road to Damascus, when the King of Heaven shone around him and asked, "Why are you persecuting Me?" (Acts 9:4), Paul fell to the ground before Him, and the entire trajectory of his life changed. Wuest continues,

> All this Paul left to become a poor itinerant missionary. But not only did he forfeit all this when he was saved, but his parents would have nothing to do with a son who had in their estimation dishonored them by becoming one of those hated, despised Christians. They had reared him in the lap of luxury, had sent him to the Jewish school of theology in Jerusalem to sit at the feet of the great Gamaliel, and had given him an excellent training in Greek culture at the University of Tarsus, a Greek school of learning. But they had now cast him off. He was still forfeiting all that he had held dear, what for? He tells us, "that I may win Christ." (Wuest 2015)

It is here that we reach the crux of Paul's point. Though he might boast of his lineage, of his birthright, of his upbringing and education, of his righteousness in the Law, he has come to know that such boasting would be utterly empty, devoid of any meaning, because it is all worthless. So, he casts away those things which have the trappings of meaning without the substance, like white bread which fills the stomach but does not satisfy the body. He turns away from all that made him who he had been up to that point, seeking the bread of Life, rich, hearty, and satisfying for the body as well as the soul. It is a great sacrifice.

When we asked the women of our group if they had been persecuted for their faith, in the way that Saul had once persecuted the Church of Christ, the way that Paul describes "suffering the loss of all things," many women shook their heads, and one even went so far as to state that she didn't believe such persecution existed in America today. Another woman, however, spoke up. She is a Messianic Jew and she described how her family had utterly rejected her after she found Jesus. She spoke movingly of the pain of ostracism, of the culture of Judaism, so focused on the importance of family, and her exile from them. Her pain was poignant and her point valid. Perhaps we are not beaten and whipped, stoned and crucified, but we face persecution, nonetheless, for our choice to follow Christ. As Paul lost his honor, his position, and his family, so, too, do we risk all when we choose to turn to Christ, alone.

However, there is hope, here, too, which cannot be ignored. Paul takes all that he was, all that he had been born into and all that he had earned through earthly work and effort, and he tosses it aside as rubbish. Yet, God uses it, as He always seems to when we cast ourselves upon His altar. God leverages that sacrifice into one of the most potent defenses of Gentile Christianity. If Paul, a student of the Old Testament, a chief Jew among Jews, would welcome the Gentiles into the fold of Jesus' flock, who could oppose him? And if Paul, who has learned the value of faith over works, of "the righteousness which comes from God" over "a righteousness of my own derived from the Law," would share that with all those who believed, regardless of how they were born or raised, who could hope to deny him?

Join In Following My Example

Philippians 3 builds from start to finish, each point emphasizing the one previous and climbing to a crashing crescendo, making it very difficult to break into bite-sized pieces. Please keep this in mind as we move from Philippians 3:9 to Philippians 3:10-21, which are divided by only a single comma, not even a period or a paragraph break, arbitrary though those sometimes are. Remember where Paul is coming from, warning against Judaizers and following up with his assurance of what the true circumcision looks like. Remember, too, how he takes the bite out of their teeth by pointing to the futility of the righteousness of man, focusing instead on the righteousness which is of God and reflecting what he wrote in Philippians 2:13, "for it is God who is at work in you." As Paul leaves behind that which he has cast aside, the rubbish, the false righteousness, and the Law, he moves now into that which he would gain.

Philippians 3:10-15

One of the things that I love about Paul is the way he challenges our expectations of what it means to be a Christian at every turn. Having cast all of the aforementioned aside, one might expect that he would cap his point with an eloquent flourish, illustrating the glory in store for those who choose Christ. Instead, he presents a very different list. We will know Him, of course, and there is power in His resurrection that we will also share in, but, more importantly, we will also fellowship in His suffering and conform to His death. You will remember Paul wrote earlier, saying, "For to you it has also been granted for Christ's sake, not only to believe in Him, but also to suffer for His sake" (Philippians 1:29). If I'm being honest, that doesn't exactly sound appealing.

When I take a moment to truly think about what these verses promise, I find I almost shrink in fear. What does the fellowship of Christ's sufferings entail? What did His death look like? Scorned and rejected at every turn, Jesus said, "The foxes have holes and the birds of the air have nests, but the Son of Man has nowhere to lay His head" (Luke 9:58). The prophet Isaiah said of him, "He was despised and forsaken of men, a man of sorrows and acquainted with grief; and like one from whom men hide their face He was despised, and we did not esteem Him" (Isaiah 53:3). Indeed, in the previous verses, Paul has already explained what we ought to expect in following Jesus. Yet, it is hard to count the things of this world as rubbish: the relationships, the safety and security, and the complacency that we so often fall prey to.

And, as if the fellowship of His sufferings isn't enough, then Paul says we will also be conformed to Jesus' death. Having studied the medical aspects of the crucifixion in excruciating detail, I can say with utter certainty that I hope never to experience the like. What is his point, then? Perhaps Paul hopes to weed out the timorous, the meek, the fearful, lukewarm Christians alluded to in Revelation 3:16. Perhaps he hopes only to warn us that trials will come, and that Jesus promises neither safety nor security, but a far greater reward: the resurrection from the dead. If we are conformed to Jesus in both suffering and death, does it not then follow that we shall also be conformed to Him in life and in His resurrection? And, if we deny being conformed to the former, does it not then follow that we should be denied the latter?

One of the things I am learning about right now is the reciprocity inherent in close relationships. To create true authenticity and intimacy one must be vulnerable, one must be truthful, one must be willing to allow the give and take of compromise and the vagaries of the human experience. I cannot give less than that and expect deep and abiding friendships to appear; I cannot refuse to bring my real self and yet expect to be known. Our relationship with Jesus is the same, though magnified by the fact that He can see our inmost being, knows every thought before we voice it, knows every vice and virtue, though we hide it from the world. Sharing in His resurrection, then, only comes through the real, authentic relationship that we build through sharing in His suffering and death. The blessing will always, and only, come when we are willing to embrace the challenge, as well.

Such a calling seems beyond our human abilities, to be honest; yet Jesus meets us. Remember, Paul began by saying, "that I may know Him." Knowing Him, by definition and reciprocity, means that He, too, will know us – utterly, completely, intimately. The word Paul uses here, *ginōskō* (BLB 2016, Strong's G1097), in fact, can also be translated as *understand* or *perceive*, and is the same word used to describe the relationship between a husband and wife, implying the same level of intimacy between Christ and ourselves. And it is a good thing that He knows us this well, for it is only in this level of intimate knowledge that He can also work in us.

Once again, Paul alludes to Philippians 2:13, where he wrote, "for it is God who is at work in you, both to will and to work for His good pleasure." Philippians 3:12 returns to this theme and Paul expands on it, describing in the following verses how perfection is a goal that ought to be sought after, but has not yet been attained and, short of the Cross, shall not be attained during our time here on this earthly plane.

Nevertheless, the "prize of the upward call" is clear. Remember in Philippians 1, Paul said, "For I am confident of this very thing, that He who began a good work in you will perfect it until the day of Christ Jesus" (Philippians 1:6). Later, Paul expanded this theme in Philippians 2:12-13. Finally, he brings it full circle here as he explains that perfection has not yet been attained, and likely never will be, yet the higher calling of Christ Jesus is sufficient. He says, "I press on so that I may lay hold of that for which also I was laid hold of by Christ Jesus" (Philippians 3:12). Guzik explains, "This is an important idea; yet sometimes Christians react to that idea by being passive. They suppose, 'Jesus got a hold of me; so that is it now. I am a Christian and I am going to heaven.' Paul showed a different attitude, that he would take hold for that for which Jesus took hold of him" (Guzik 2006c). Guzik goes on to powerfully illustrate this idea of constantly pressing on. He says,

> When Spain led the world (in the 15th century), their coins reflected their national arrogance and were inscribed *Ne Plus Ultra* which meant "Nothing Further" – meaning that Spain was the ultimate in all the world. After the discovery of the New World, they realized that they were not the end of the world, so they changed the inscription on

their coinage to *Plus Ultra* meaning 'More Beyond.' In the same pattern, some Christian lives say, 'Nothing Further' and others say "More Beyond." (Guzik 2006c)

So, Paul explains, "forgetting what lies behind and reaching forward to what lies ahead, I press on" (Philippians 3:13-14).

Paul's life clearly says *Plus Ultra*, "More Beyond," and he calls the Philippians to join him. He challenges them further, though, not content to simply share his own example (see verse 17), but to call them to the same high ideal. It is a convicting challenge to read today. "Let us therefore, as many as are perfect, have this attitude" (Philippians 3:15). I admit, I was at first confounded by this. On the one hand, Paul, himself, admits his imperfection, his utter reliance on God to work in him, the fact that he has not yet obtained perfect fellowship with Christ Jesus. Yet, on the other, only a few verses later, he drops this bombshell. On the surface, it could, perhaps, be meant in a mocking manner. *Oh, you who are perfect, remember how imperfect you actually are*; and I don't know that to read it as such would be wrong. Yet, as I study and ask for the wisdom of the Holy Spirit, I sense a deeper meaning, one that Paul will allude to in just a moment. I think what Paul suggests here is that there is, in fact, a certain perfection in being imperfect. We are created beings, forged from mud and breathed into life by the very essence of the Divine Creator. We are perfect even in our imperfections, and the greatest perfection we could seek is to live each day seeking greater communion with that by which we were created. Paul is not saying that only those who are perfect, or perfected, ought to have this attitude, but that this is the perfect attitude to have towards Jesus.

Paul completes these verses with one final point of note. He reminds his readers of the importance of spiritual discernment and prayer. One can hardly read a single letter of Paul's without fully apprehending his deep and abiding commitment to the discipline of prayer. In Ephesians, he says, "With all prayer and petition, pray at all times in the Spirit" (Ephesians 6:18). In 1 Thessalonians, he says, "Pray without ceasing" (1 Thessalonians 5:17). In 2 Corinthians, he exhorts, "Test yourselves to see if you are in the faith; examine yourselves!" (2 Corinthians 13:5). This echoes David's plea in Psalms, "Search me, O God, and know my heart; try me and know my anxious thoughts; and see if there be any hurtful way in me, and lead me in the everlasting way" (Psalm 139:23-24). I love this prayer because it reminds us that God is able to convict, to mend, to reconcile, so long as we are open to His influence. The Holy Spirit does not speak condemnation, but He will speak reproof. Wise is the man who receives such instruction, or, as Proverbs says, "Reprove a wise man and he will love you. Give instruction to a wise man and he will be still wiser" (Proverbs 9:8-9).

Philippians 3:16-21

Paul is, himself, perhaps the greatest example of those whom he now warns against. Remembering his power and prestige, his zeal and righteousness before the Law, there is no one better positioned than he to deliver this warning. For it was in his previous life as Saul that he might have just as easily ended in destruction, whose appetite for power and the things of the earth may have consumed him as a false god, and who gloried in his greatest shame: the persecution of the Church of Christ. He recognized those he describes in this chapter because he was one such person, before Jesus got hold of him and transformed him, before he was made new, perfected in Christ, and sent forth upon his great calling. So it is, too, that in being the greatest example of this type of person, he can also promise the utter transformation that Jesus offers those who believe.

Yet, Paul also wept for those he describes here. I think it's interesting to note that Paul is not often recorded as weeping, even chastising those in Caesarea, "What are you doing, weeping and breaking my heart?" (Acts 21:13) when they fear for his safety in Jerusalem. He did not weep at the death of Stephen or the many others whose lives he had taken as he ravaged the early church. He did not weep when shipwrecked, when bound and chained, nor when beaten and imprisoned. Yet, his heart breaks here for those so like himself, yet so far removed from any hope of redemption. I'm reminded of the adage, "Lord, break my heart for the things that break Yours." Paul wept seeing their destruction and showed us yet one more example of how we ought to live: weeping for the enemies of Christ, who know Him not, and who will be destroyed for their lack. Indeed, our hearts ought to break for them, for their enmity is not with us, but with God, Himself, who will "[give] them over to the stubbornness of their heart, to walk in their own devices" (Psalm 81:12).

However, if we live as Paul has described; if we press on; if we follow his example and the example of those like him, turning away from the destruction of Judaizers and false teachers, the complacency of our worldly riches, and the false glories that lead us only to shame; and if we remember our citizenship in Heaven, then there is, indeed, a great prize forthcoming. As he promised in verse 11, it is only in being conformed to the likeness of Jesus Christ in His suffering and death that we can be conformed to His image in His resurrection.

While there is neither time nor space here to devote to what that resurrection might look like, I think it suffices to say that it is all but unknowable. Paul says, "by the exertion of the power that He has," offering no further explanation. Perhaps our best guess at this resurrection is found in Revelation 21, where the apostle John describes the new heaven and earth and the new Jerusalem. Yet even this can be only a pale reflection of the glory Jesus has in store for us who believe, and while we may not know the fullness of the details, it is enough for me, at least, to cling to His promise of glory.

In the Lord

Finally, we reach Paul's last words to the Philippians. Yet, even here, he continues to teach, to exhort, and to encourage. I have really struggled with how to present this chapter, then, because it is both a continuation of Paul's rich teaching and a concluding statement, drawing together the rich threads of the tapestry he has thus far woven. To approach it as one precludes the opportunity to experience the other, and vice versa. Then too, both are mutually exclusive of the beauty of Paul's writings as a whole across multiple letters, which follow many of the same themes, such as rejoicing, living well, reliance on God, his ministry to the Gentiles, and the rejection of the false circumcision.

With all of this in mind, I want to take a two-fold approach to the concluding chapter of Philippians, studying it both as a continuation of his teaching and also as the conclusion it is meant to be. As we consider each section, then, remember what has come before, what Paul has already preached and is continuing to preach, and think about how his points here fit within the larger, sweeping framework of his entire epistle. Please begin with the warm affection we find Paul expressing to his dear friends in Philippians 4:1-9.

Philippians 4:1-3

Having concluded Philippians 3 with a rousing challenge to live on this earthly plane as if we are Citizens of Heaven, fully expecting to suffer with Christ but also sharing in His glorification, Paul exhorts the Philippians to three further behaviors: "stand firm," "live in harmony," and, in verse 4, "rejoice." All of these should be done "in the Lord," which bears out further both Paul's theme of Chapter 3, as well as Swift's theory that all of Philippians should be read through the lens of their participation in the gospel, both with Paul and with God.

As he calls them to stand firm, Paul honeys his words with such warm affection that it is impossible to miss his genuine care and devotion to his dear friends at Philippi. He calls them "brethren," "fellow workers," and, in a single sentence, refers to them twice as "beloved." Perhaps you have such a bosom friend as Paul describes here, a twin soul that is as dear to you as your own. Maybe it is a spouse, a sibling, a parent, or simply a friend, who is the family of your heart. If you are so lucky, perhaps you can identify with Paul's tone in these verses.

Yet, Paul does not refer to a single person, but to an entire church; the entire community of believers at Philippi is as dear to his heart as himself. So, too, are those believers at Rome (Roman 12:19) and Corinth (1 Corinthians 4:14, 10:14, 15:58; 2 Corinthians 7:1, 12:19), as well as dozens of individuals named throughout his writings. Of course, we can never forget Timothy, most beloved of Paul, son and fellow teacher. More, though, Paul uses this word in a very deliberate fashion, as he shows in its many other usages across his writing in which he uses it to refer to us – the True Circumcision – as "beloved" of God (Romans 1:7; Ephesians 1:6, 5:1; Colossians 3:12; 1 Thessalonians 2:13). Further, he uses it as an homage to God's own term for Jesus, His son. Matthew, Mark, and Luke all record the voice of the Lord declaring, "This is my beloved son, with whom I am well-pleased." Thus, we are beloved of Paul, beloved of God, and beloved like Jesus, Himself, was beloved of His Holy Father.

Yet, Paul goes further, calling the Philippians not only beloved, but also his joy and crown. While this marks Paul's fifth usage of *joy* in his letter to Philippi, perhaps it is his reference here to a crown that is more of note. The word used in this instance is *stephanos* (BLB 2016, Strong's G4735), which refers to a crown of victory, similar to those used to crown ancient Greek Olympians, a practice that continues today. In 2 Timothy, Paul says, "I have fought the good fight, I have finished the course, I have kept the faith" (2 Timothy 4:7). Other versions translate it as, "I have finished the race." In either case, this would have been a commonly understood metaphor for Paul's audience. What is less obvious is that this is also the same word used to describe the woven crown of thorns placed on Jesus' head during his crucifixion.

This two-fold crowning is exceedingly symbolic, then, referring not only to the victory of believers and Christ's victory over death and sin, but also to remind his readers, once again, that their victory did not come without cost. When Paul calls them his crown, he reminds them both that they are victorious *in* Christ, and also that they are victorious *because of* Christ. Likewise, they ought to expect to receive a similar two-fold crown in their own lives: one which is both prize and prudence, a reminder that they have won, but also that their participation in the gospel, their suffering with Christ, should never be far from their hearts and minds.

I find this symbolism so powerful for another reason, as well. We see in Matthew, "And after twisting together a crown of thorns, they put it on His head, and a reed in His right hand; and they knelt down before Him and mocked Him, saying, 'Hail, King of the Jews!'" (Matthew 27:29). What those who persecuted Christ meant for mockery, we know stood for truth: the truth of his kingship, the truth of his Godhood, and the truth of his death and resurrection for our sakes. How often does God take what the world intended for ill and use it for His glory? It is even a fitting symbol for Paul, himself: a man being used to persecute the Church of God, making a mockery of those who worshipped the Son, then realizing the truth of the everlasting God. God often subverts the purposes of the enemy to His own ends.

Yet, even as Paul encourages and exhorts the Philippians, he has a special warning for two of their body. Indeed, it is difficult to miss this small aside, but, without context, it is also easy to breeze right past it. In his second "in the Lord," Paul reminds Euodia and Syntyche to "live in harmony." Who are these women (because it is believed that both are feminine names), and what is their relevance? To answer these questions, we must first remember that women have had a founding role in the Church at Philippi from its beginning. On the banks of a nearby river, a young Paul preached the gospel to a small group; Lydia, in faith, believed, becoming the first European convert and beginning the very first European church in her home. To lend further context, it is important to understand that Macedonian women, unlike their Greek or Roman counterparts, were not consigned to home and hearth. Barclay explains,

> It is very interesting to see women playing so leading a part in the affairs of one of the early congregations for in Greece women remained very much in the background. It was the aim of the Greeks that a respectable woman should "see as little, hear as little and ask as little as possible." A respectable woman never appeared on the street alone; she had her own apartments in the house and never joined the male members of the family even for meals. Least of all had she any part in public life. But Philippi was in Macedonia, and in Macedonia things were very different. There women had a freedom and a place which they had nowhere in the rest of Greece. In Thessalonica many of the chief women were won for Christianity, and the same happened in Berea (Ac.17:4,12). The evidence of inscriptions points the same way. A wife erects a tomb for herself and for her husband out of their joint earnings, so she must have been in business. We even find monuments erected to women by public bodies. We know that in many of the Pauline Churches (for example, in Corinth), women had to be content with a very subordinate place. But it is well worth remembering, when we are thinking of the place of women in the early Church and of Paul's attitude to them, that in the Macedonian Churches they clearly had a leading place. (Barclay 1959, 90)

With this in mind, it is easy to see why most commentators agree that these two women, Euodia and Syntyche, were likely women of import in the Philippian church, perhaps even some of Paul's original converts and leaders of small home churches within the larger Philippian community. As such, it is unlikely these women are of the petty, divisive, mean-spirited nature that Paul warned against at the beginning of Philippians 3, saying, "Beware of the dogs, beware of the evil workers, beware of the false circumcision" (Philippians 3:2). Paul, himself, suggests otherwise, saying they "have shared my struggle in the cause of the gospel" (Philippians 4:3). Nevertheless, even the most God-fearing of worshippers, those of the "true circumcision," can have specious, even ridiculous disagreements with one another. The enemy loves to use our human nature against us and against the work of God.

Of course, we know absolutely nothing about this type of disagreement, right? I love how Patricia Shirer describes it, calling it "heated fellowship" (Shirer 2015). What a delightfully euphemistic phrase for the kind of petty disagreements that arise between believers. Recently, our church underwent a period of transition that included several staff members either choosing to leave or being asked to leave. As we grieved, there was a sense among our community that this ought not to have happened within a church. Perhaps they are right; our commonality in Christ ought to overshadow any pettiness between us. Yet, as I am often reminded, we are not a community of Saints (though we are a community of *saints*), and our fallen nature means that we are as likely to be trapped by our humanity as any non-believer. Or, as my husband quipped, "Ain't no mess like a church mess."

In any case, Paul calls on these two women to settle their differences and calls upon the entire community at Philippi to help them to do so. Barclay observes,

> It is significant that when there was a quarrel at Philippi, Paul mobilized the whole resources of the Church to mend it. He thought no effort too great to maintain the peace of the Church. A quarrelling Church is no Church at all, for it is one from which Christ has been shut out. No man can be at peace with God and at variance with his fellow-men. (Barclay 1959, 91)

It is interesting to note that when Paul calls them to "live in harmony," he uses a term that I hope you will remember from our study of Philippians 2: *phroneō*, which denoted utter unity of mind and purpose. Paul uses this word to reinforce what he has already said, "make my joy complete by being of the same mind, maintaining the same love, united in spirit, intent on one purpose" (Philippians 2:2), or, as we transliterated these words earlier, "united in unity, purposed on one purpose."

It is sad to see such women of God accorded only a single line of text yet remembered through the ages in this way. They stand a lesson to us across history, as does their counterpart, Clement, remembered for just the opposite; and as many commentators, including Guzik, have noted, "If you had to have your whole life summed up in one sentence, would you like it to be summed up like Clement or like Euodia and Syntyche?" (Guzik 2006d). While I certainly strive for the former, I'm ever grateful for the grace and mercy of the cross, which promises forgiveness for those moments of "heated fellowship" that are so much more like the latter.

Philippians 4:4-7

As a further balm to divisiveness, Paul continues by repeating (and repeating) one of his central themes: rejoice! Spurgeon says,

> I am glad that we do not know what the quarrel was about; I am usually thankful for ignorance on such subjects; – but as a cure for disagreements, the apostle says, 'Rejoice in the Lord always.' People who are very happy, especially those who are very happy in the Lord, are not apt either to give offense or to take offense. Their minds are so sweetly occupied with higher things, that they are not easily distracted by the little troubles which naturally arise among such imperfect creatures as we are. Joy in the Lord is the cure for all discord. (Spurgeon 1895)

As joy brings contentment in even the most trying of circumstances, rejoicing can bring unity to our petty divisions.

Not only joy and rejoicing, but a "gentle spirit" can also act as a panacea against disagreement. This is an interesting phrase to try to translate, rife with complications in understanding what it connotes. *Epieikēs* (BLB 2016, Strong's G1933) in the Greek, Strong's suggests *mild, moderate, gentle,* or *patient.* However, a cursory side-by-side reading of even a few versions will show that translators have long struggled with how to maintain its meaning within an English context. The New International Version (NIV) uses "gentleness," the New Living Translation (NLT) says "considerate," the English Standard Version (ESV) says "reasonableness," the King James Version (KJV) uses "moderation," the HCSB uses "graciousness," and on and on. What, then, does this phrase really mean? Even commentators disagree. Guzik suggests, "This word describes the heart of a person who will let the Lord fight his battles. They know that 'vengeance is Mine, says the Lord' (Romans 12:19). It describes a person who is really free to let go of His anxieties and all the things that cause him stress, because he knows that the Lord will take up his cause" (Guzik 2006d). Whereas, Barclay says,

> The Greeks themselves explained this word as "justice and something better than

> justice." They said that *epieikeia* (GSN1932) ought to come in when strict justice became unjust because of its generality. There may be individual instances where a perfectly just law becomes unjust or where justice is not the same thing as equity. A man has the quality of *epieikeia* (GSN1932) if he knows when not to apply the strict letter of the law, when to relax justice and introduce mercy. (Barclay 1959, 93)

While Guzik might present a more modern context, I can't help but appreciate Barclay's primary source material, using the Greeks' own words to help describe this concept; and, as I read it, I can't help but think that it is this, exactly, that Christ came to do. He abolished the Law and brought mercy and love. He brought accountability tempered by grace. He brought conviction with reconciliation. The Lord is, indeed, near. No longer far off, unattainable for those outside the priesthood, but intimate and personal, known and knowing.

It is this very concept that allows forgiveness from God, and allows us to forgive others their shortcomings, once again diffusing the tension of petty disagreement. It brings the understanding that perfect justice isn't always perfect. When my son doesn't get his way and throws a temper tantrum, it is *epieikēs* that allows me to understand that he is exhausted, or hungry, or overwrought from too busy a day, and enfold him in a grounding hug rather than extracting punishment. It is *epieikēs* that helps me to remember that not everyone has the same opportunities that I have, and they are doing the best they can with what they've got. Rather than judging the single mom who works full time for not having better behaved children, it is *epieikēs* that allows me to see her with grace and mercy, a fellow sufferer for Christ's sake, doing the best that she can with what she has been given. It makes me a better mother, a better wife, a better friend, and a better person.

It is interesting to me that Paul's line, then, "The Lord is near," can either be attached to this preceding statement, or to the one following it. It works either way, rather like a Wheel of Fortune Before & After puzzle. It can be read, "Let your gentle spirit be known to all men. The Lord is near," or "The Lord is near. Be anxious for nothing." Which does it belong with? I like to think that the answer is both. Be kind to others, give them the benefit of the doubt, love them first, before judging them, because this is what God has done for you. And also, because he has done this for you, do not be overcome by fear and anxiety; He is with you.

I am a worrier. 'Tis the curse, I suppose, of a firstborn, type A, control-freak personality. Not only do I worry about things I can't control and things in the future, I worry about the things of the past, turning them over and over again in my brain, wishing I would have spoken or acted differently and worrying what impact my choices will have. I have no sense of "water under the bridge" or "shake it off" and I have no ability to relax, saying "*que sera sera*" (what will be will be). I suppose, at the least, it means I'm not fatalistic.

As a new Christian, Matthew 6:25-34 spent many years being my life verses. It was an ever-present reminder that my worrying had no purpose. As I've grown and matured, however, I've learned that it is not enough to create a vacuum in my mind where the worry once resided; it inevitably creeps back in. On the other hand, Paul reminds us to fill that space with other considerations. He juxtaposes the "nothing" for which we ought to be anxious with the "everything" by which we are to pray and petition God, garnishing it with a healthy helping of gratitude, as well. *The Message* is unique in describing these verses. "Don't fret or worry. Instead of worrying, pray. Let petitions and praises shape your worries into prayers, letting God know your concerns" (Philippians 4:6, *The Message*). I love the visual of our prayers being shaped with the fluidity of a master potter shaping a bowl or cup from wet clay. As when Paul wrote to the Romans, "In the same way the Spirit also helps our weakness; for we do not know how to pray as we should, but the Spirit Himself intercedes for us with groanings too deep for words" (Romans 8:26), our prayers are shaped by both word and Spirit, by the intent of our minds and desires of our hearts.

Yet, Paul does not stop there. In a sweeping declaration, he promises that those who do this, those who overcome anxiety with prayer, who rest in thanksgiving, will receive, in return, the peace of God. And not only the peace of God, but an absolute peace, the kind of peace that so overwhelms our circumstances that there is no reasonable explanation for it. It is the peace that allows the terminally ill patient to rest easy in God's perfect plan, the terrified flyer to set foot on an airplane, the anxious parent to sleep through the night, even as their child is far from their protective embrace.

Incidentally, the word used here for "thanksgiving" is *eucharistia* (BLB 2016, Strong's G2169), where our word *eucharist* comes from – the ceremony of remembrance we participate in out of thanksgiving for Christ's sacrifice on the cross. In the very word, itself, then, we are being reminded that the ultimate cost has already been paid. Unimaginable though it may be, we already have credit in God's eyes, as Abraham, to whom "He credited it to him as righteousness" (Genesis 15:6, HCSB). If we but ask, Christ's sacrifice has already made a way for God to respond. And not just respond, but to overwhelm us. "'Test me now in this,' says the Lord of hosts, 'if I will not open for you the windows of heaven and pour out for you a blessing until it overflows,'" (Malachi 3:10b), He promises. I particularly love the NIV translation of this verse: "See if I will not throw open the floodgates of heaven and pour out so much blessing that there will not be room enough to store it." He promises His response will not be faint but will overcome us in its blessing!

Perhaps it is fatalistic, in a sense, to trust in God to such an extent that one's belief in His ultimate faithfulness relieves every iota of good sense we might claim to possess; however, as a chronic worrier, I can't help but breathe a little easier every time He overwhelms my mind with His tender presence. Not only will He cover me with peace, but He will further fill in the spaces in my own mind, guarding me from future worry and anxiety. In my Bible, I have this note: "Pray, and be at peace." It is done.

Philippians 4:8-9

As if filling our minds with thanksgiving and the balm of God's peace isn't enough, Paul goes on to list a number of other things on which we ought to fix our thoughts. I admit, because of my worrying nature, this list acts as a touch point for me. Writing it on my bathroom mirror with a dry erase marker gives me a visual reminder throughout my day not only to empty my mind of worry and concern, but also to fill it with higher pursuits. And, when I'm being less than successful and find myself going round in circles, fixating on the negative, it gives the Spirit form by which to nudge me out of my negative thought patterns. Instead of whining about how difficult caring for a toddler can be, I'm reminded that I'm being honored to raise a child of God. Instead of listing all the things about my husband that have disappointed me lately, I instead list all the ways he shows he loves me.

While the NASB offers "true," "honorable," "right," "pure," "lovely," "good repute," "excellence," and "praise worthy," it is worth noting that other translations can help us flesh out the actual meaning of these things. The NIV mentions "noble" and "admirable;" the ESV uses "commendable;" the KJV uses "honest" and "virtuous;" the HCSB uses "moral excellence;" and the ABPE offers "precious" and "glorious." Imagine, then, if we committed ourselves to contemplating each of these concepts for just a few minutes each day.

Yet, what does it mean to "dwell" on these things? Interestingly, this is more of an accounting term than one of *meditating* or *inhabiting*. It is also one that supports the idea of logical deduction. Even the Greek word, *logizomai* (BLB 2016, Strong's G3049), seems to imply a relationship to our modern word, *logic*. Similar uses include *think, impute, reckon, count, account, suppose, reason,* and *number*. Guzik says,

Much of the Christian life comes down to the mind. Romans 12:2 speaks of the essential place of "being transformed by the renewing of your mind" and 2 Corinthians 10:5 speaks of the importance of "casting down arguments and every high thing that exalts itself against the knowledge of God, bringing every thought into captivity to the obedience of Christ." What we choose to meditate on matters. (Guzik 2006d)

This is not always easy to do. Years into the challenge of caring for a terminally ill husband, unwell, herself, one of our women came forward while studying these verses and shared this powerful testimony:

> Focus. *The Lord is near.* His presence is a gentle reminder of His grace and love.
> Stop hand wringing, rocking in the worry chair that goes nowhere, and pray. My prayer is so repetitive: help. My supplication is: help. My thanksgiving is: help. My requests are simple, and I let God know. He promises peace, which like a centurion, stands guard over our hearts and our minds. In this turmoil, I often don't feel the deep abiding peace I have known in my decades of knowing God's love. But I walk by faith not feelings.
> So move on. Don't get stuck.
> *Finally, brethren. Whatever is true.* The truth looks ugly. I see paralysis, slurred speech, death and destruction.
> Move on.

Whatever is honorable. Nope! No honor or dignity in the daily routine of caring for ALS. Not only does my husband have ALS but when we were diagnosed I was told, WE have ALS. I feel less dignified, more unbalanced even after years of teaching others how to have firm footing in the Word of God.

Move on.

Whatever is right? But everything feels SO wrong, so upside down. And I helplessly stand by; the many gifts God has given me seem paltry in my serving.

Move on.

Whatever is pure. I want to puke as I watch the ugliness creep into lives. Focus.   Focus. Focus.

Whatever is lovely, soft, kind, winsome, gentle has been stolen from our life. Nope. Nothing here to think about. I push it from my mind.

Move on.

Whatever is of good repute, attractive, has reputation is not in the definition of ALS, not in the manuals. No good ending.

Move on. Don't mull.

If there is any excellence. I am halted in my pity and here the Lord who is excellent, good, filled with joy for the road set before him steps into my prayer. He who endured the suffering and humiliation of the cross focused on eternity and the fruit of his suffering.

If there is anything worthy of praise. It is God. I praise Him, sing songs of praise stored in my Holy Spirit radio that plays all day long. Sometimes volume and beat pumped up, sometimes crooning soft words of comfort. But it is praise that I can give to my Lord.

These are the things my mind is told to dwell on. *Let the morning bring me word of your unfailing love, for I have put my trust in You.* I write these words on my kitchen window that greets the sunrise. (CK 2015)

Her powerful words reminded us all that there are deep and terrible things facing those who walk in Christ each and every day, burdens too heavy to conceivably bear. And yet, God is good.

Fortunately, Paul understands this burden, this battle. In Ephesians he writes, "For our struggle is not against flesh and blood but against the rulers, against the powers, against the world forces of this darkness, against the spiritual forces of wickedness in the heavenly places" (Ephesians 6:12). It is these verses that also refer to putting on the full armor of God, including the belt of truth, the breastplate of righteousness, the shoes of peace, the shield of faith, the helmet of salvation, and the sword of the Spirit, all of which are anchored in prayer. If you have been paying attention, you should be able to quickly identify all of these pieces of armor in Paul's message to the Philippians. Paul's writing does not change. We are at war, yes, and the battlefield, as Joyce Meyer writes, is in our minds, but we are victorious in Him "who is greater than he who is in the world" (1 John 4:4, NIV).

Further, Paul gives himself as an example, saying that we have "learned and received and heard and seen" in him all of these. When I first read this verse, I couldn't help but think of the symmetry of these words and their symbolism. From a teacher we may learn and hear, but it is only by the Spirit that we may receive and truly see. As I dug deeper, I was reminded of how often God offers wisdom to the one who asks; and Jesus, himself, was called Rabbi, or *teacher*. He even promised, "But the Helper, the Holy Spirit, whom the Father will send in My name, He will teach you all things, and bring to your remembrance all that I said to you" (John 14:26). We have been given a teacher in Paul, an example to follow, and we have been given a Teacher in the Holy Spirit, a divine discerner who will help us fight these battles. Then, being victorious, we are offered another beautiful symmetry: not only the "peace of God" (v. 4:7) within us, but also the "God of peace" (v. 4:9) beside us.

The Grace of the Lord Jesus Christ Be with You

As we reach Paul's final few paragraphs to the Philippians, how I wish we could sit together and read again the whole of Philippians. I hope that as we study his words, you are able to see not only the individual threads of his thoughts, but also the whole picture, which transcends any single concept. In fact, Paul's writing is so divinely inspired, so filled with grace and truth, I hope you will return to it again and again. While any single verse can offer the kind of trite advice that so easily drips from our lips, it is only by studying the whole of the Word that we can discern God's heart for us. The enemy seeks to deceive us, using the very word of God against Him. As Spurgeon is purported to have said, "Discernment is not simply a matter of telling the difference between what is right and wrong; rather it is the difference between right and *almost* right." It is only in submitting ourselves to the whole of God's word, not just a few verses here and there, that we can, by the Spirit, discern the difference.

Let us, then, one final time, pray before we read. *Heavenly Father, what a journey you have led us on together. We are so grateful for this time spent immersing ourselves in Your Word and continue to ask for wisdom. By the Spirit, please reveal Your ways to us as we read and study, not simply as children do, but with all the complexity and maturity of Christ-followers, Citizens of Heaven, saints, as those in Philippi before us. Amen.* Please, then, return to Philippians one final time and read Philippians 4:10-23.

Philippians 4:10-14

My husband and I are college sweethearts. We met during our freshman year (when my roommate had a crush on him), and our friendship grew slowly. Eventually, my roommate moved on, but he and I remained fast friends. So much so, in fact, that by the time we went on our first date, everyone around us breathed a sigh of relief. *Finally!* (Perhaps the irony was that I didn't even know it was a date until long after the fact.) We were married at the end of our junior year with less than $100 in our newly combined bank account and spent three more quarters in the university Married Student Housing. We were full-time students, but there were also bills to pay. Between us, we worked at least three, often four or five jobs, plus studying, classes, and internships. Every month, we would sit in front of a big desk calendar and write in each bill we were expecting on the date it would come due. We would also pencil in each paycheck and the expected amount. Using this, we would create a monthly budget and calendar that would allow us to pay each bill without becoming delinquent. If it didn't look like we were going to make it, both of us would pick up some extra hours.

    I remember the worst job my husband ever held. We were living in Texas in the height of the summer, and he worked the late shift electro-chemical polishing surgical equipment for veterinary use. It involved wearing a full Tyvek hazmat suit in an enclosed lab, often well over 100 degrees. He would load razor-sharp screws into a plastic tray, dip it into a vat of hot acid, wait a prescribed period of time, then move it to the next vat of acid, then the next one, each one weaker than the last, before finally rinsing them and setting them to dry. The tips would tear through his gloves, so by the time he came home his skin would be dotted with pin pricks of red-hot, acid-irritated cuts. He held that job for six months, during some of the most desperate early days of our marriage. Later, he found out that he had lasted well over twice as long as any previous employee.

    Even with this income, we often struggled to make ends meet. We were always adequately fed, but there was never any extra. I remember one Thanksgiving when we were gifted not one, not two, but three turkeys. How excited we were! We stretched that meat to last all the way until Christmas break, when we could go home and be fed by our families instead. To this day, I hate the taste of turkey.

What allowed my husband to daily subject himself to such misery? What allowed us to find joy and peace in the midst of such challenge? Perhaps it was simply the glow of newly wedded bliss. But perhaps, it was as Paul says, "I can do all things through Him who strengthens me." We had to learn contentment or be content in our misery. Either way, it involved finding some composure in the midst of what could easily become overwhelming circumstances.

In the previous verse, Paul exhorted the Philippians to "practice" that which he had been preaching and demonstrating. Now he says, "I have learned to be content in whatever circumstances I am" (Philippians 4:11). While it may seem obvious, it is worth noting that if something must be learned, it is not something that comes naturally. Translated from the Greek word *manthanō* (BLB 2016, Strong's G3129), it has a very specific meaning, including "to learn by use and practice; to be in the habit of, accustomed to." Paul has not miraculously been graced with Godly contentment; he has chosen it. As when he and Silas chose to rejoice in the Philippian prison a decade before, it is by deliberate and conscious effort that he has since developed this ability.

Paul writes to Timothy, "But godliness actually is a means of great gain when accompanied by contentment. For we have brought nothing into this world, so we cannot take anything out of it either. If we have food and covering, with these we shall be content" (1 Timothy 6:6-8). Paul speaks of humble means, not even deigning to remind us of the challenges he has faced: imprisoned, beaten, shipwrecked, even! Yet, he also speaks of prosperity. God's provision is sometimes abundant, sometimes enough, sometimes short, but always, it is of God, and thus he is content to receive. At one time, God's provision was usually just enough for us, at times a bit short, yet He still provided work by which we could make up the difference. Today, many years later, we are living in a time of blessing and prosperity. The challenge, now, is to remember that enough can be plenty, in its own way. Choosing to say *enough* and being content instead of ever seeking more is its own discipline.

So it is for Paul, having received the gift of the Philippians, which, as we have already discussed, was not a deficiency in its own right, but, "lacking opportunity," it was incomplete until Epaphroditus actually arrived at Paul's home in Rome and presented him their gift. He was content before their gift, and he is content after it, remembering that all things are of God and from God. Still, Paul reminds the Philippians, again, that in sharing with him in his struggle they are, in fact, sharing in the struggle of Christ on earth.

Philippians 4:15-19

While there can be, at this point, no doubt of Paul's especial relationship with the Philippians, he reminds us one final time of their unique place in his heart and ministry. Many commentators have remarked at length that it seemed a point of pride for Paul not to accept any wages for his work within the ministry, pointing to 1 Corinthians 9:11 and 14, 2 Corinthians 11:7-9, Galatians 6:6, and, finally, 2 Thessalonians 3:8-9. These verses clearly highlight the divergence, in fact, of Paul's words and actions, fully supporting the premise that those within the ministry ought to be cared for by those whom they are serving, yet also illustrating his own preference not to do so, even going so far as to support himself by his own labor while also preaching the Word for free. Nevertheless, as his most "beloved brethren," the Philippians are the exception, not only having provided this gift, but with a long history of giving. In fact, one might almost say that they have practiced giving to Paul. I can't help but smile at this sly bit of byplay, Paul once again showing his mastery of thematic construction, linking his previous thoughts to this one. Again, too, we see Swift's theme of *participation* as Paul praises the Philippians for their diligent giving.

Nevertheless, having received the full amount of the gift from Epaphroditus, Paul makes a number of declarations or statements. One could even, perhaps, call them promises. First, he tells the Philippians that, while their gift certainly blessed him, they, themselves, were, in fact, more blessed by its giving than by his receiving. In essence, I think he is reminding us that gifts to the ministry bless the giver as much as, if not more than, the recipient. Like the tithe, a gift or offering is an act of faith, believing that by the giver's own sacrifice, God will both bless and multiply the gift, as well as provide adequate provision to the giver. In fact, as Paul described the Philippian's gift to the Church at Corinth, he wrote,

> Now brethren, we wish to make known to you the grace of God which has been given in the churches of Macedonia, that in a great ordeal of affliction their abundance of joy and their deep poverty overflowed in the wealth of their liberality. For I testify that according to their ability, and beyond their ability, they gave of their own accord, begging us with much urging for the favor of their participation in the support of the saints. (2 Corinthians 8:1-4)

While some of the Philippians were probably at least somewhat wealthy, they wouldn't have been extraordinarily so, and the majority would not have been. Their gift was a sacrifice, dearly given, for the work of the Lord and for the benefit of Paul's ministry. It is here that Paul's next promise becomes important, as he reassures them that God will, indeed, supply all their needs for their sacrifice.

Guzik calls this statement "both broad and yet restricted," pointing to Spurgeon, who used the example of the widow in 2 Kings 4:1-7 to illustrate this point. Guzik says,

> Elisha told the widow to gather empty vessels, set them out and pour forth the oil from the one small vessel of oil she had into the empty vessels. She filled and filled and miraculously filled until every empty vessel was full. *All our need* is like the empty vessels. *God* is the one who fills the empty vessels. *According to His riches in glory* describes the style in which God fills the empty vessels – the oil keeps flowing until every available vessel is filled. *By Christ Jesus* describes how God meets our needs – our empty vessels are filled with Jesus in all His glory. (Guzik 2006d)

In short, the promise is that God will supply all of one's *needs*, not *all* of one's needs. While this is a fine and delicate point, it bears repeating. Paul has already preached the importance of contentment to the Philippians, and I think that the widow's story bears this out. The vessels were filled until each was full, but the blessing ceased when that point had been reached. She did not have time, having seen the miracle of provision, to rush out and procure still more vessels. Jesus, himself, shared a similar message, saying, "Give, and it will be given to you. They will pour into your lap a good measure – pressed down, shaken together, and running over. For by your standard of measure it will be measured to you in return" (Luke 6:38).

My husband and I teach Dave Ramsey's *Financial Peace University* at our church; while our son is still quite young, only three, we're already striving to teach him good money habits, including spending wisely, saving, and having the heart of a giver. During the height of the Syrian Refugee Crisis this year, while watching a news segment on children in refugee camps, he turned to us and said, "They don't have any toys to play with. That's so sad." We agreed with him and he continued, "I'd like to give them some of my toys." Oh, the heart of a child, which sees such pain and responds so simply, yet so deeply. Never one to let a teachable moment pass us by, we commended him for this desire and, together, went to his room to retrieve his "Giving" piggy bank. We emptied it onto the table, counted the contents, and discussed how much money would be appropriate. Then, we found a reputable organization and helped him make a donation, even including in the "special notes" section that it was from our three-year-old son, and he hoped it might be used towards helping refugee children receive a toy. We believe that God blesses the giver. We believe that having the heart of a giver will help our son to be more content and more appreciative of the blessings he has received. We believe this to be true because God has said it, and because we have experienced it.

Ramsey teaches a lesson from his friend, Rabbi Daniel Lapin, who discusses the Jewish ceremony of the Havdalah Cup in his book *Thou Shall Prosper*. He says,

> The Havdalah service is recited over a cup of wine that runs over into the saucer beneath. This overflowing cup symbolizes the intention to produce during the week ahead not only sufficient to fill one's own cup, but also an excess that will allow overflow for the benefit of others. In other words, I am obliged to first fill my cup and then continue pouring as it were, so that I will have sufficient to give away to others, thus helping to jump-start their own efforts. (Lapin 2010, 150)

I think that this service would have had tremendous meaning to both Paul and to the Philippians. Like the widow of 2 Kings, once one's cup is filled, one does not replace it with a second cup or find a larger cup. It is meant to overflow. Ramsey presents this lesson with what appears to be a carafe of red wine, further cementing the visual that just as Christ's blood poured forth and overflowed, covering our sins, our overflow should, in turn, be returned to Him.

Finally, Paul refers to the gift of the Philippians as "a fragrant aroma, an acceptable sacrifice, well-pleasing to God" (Philippians 4:18). While one might not see these words as a promise at first glance, they are steeped in Old Testament tradition, lending them richness and depth, layered by God's Old Testament promises to His people. The Old Testament rules of sacrifice were extensive, varied, and exceedingly specific. Each sin required a different form of atonement; each presentation was strictly regulated; the portions for the priests, the penitent, and God, Himself, were carefully enumerated. Sacrifices could be of whole animals, a portion thereof, their blood, or of grain, wine, or fine oil. As they were consumed on the altar, the smoke would mingle with that of the golden altar of incense. In fact, Leviticus tells us, "'The priest shall also put some of the blood on the horns of the altar of fragrant incense which is before the Lord in the tent of meeting...'" (Leviticus 4:7). This incense was so carefully regulated that the Lord told Moses in Exodus, "'The incense which you shall make, you shall not make in the same portions for yourselves; it shall be holy to you for the Lord.'" (Exodus 30:37).

In fact, so prevalent is this sense of a "fragrant aroma" in the Bible that it extends from Genesis 8:21 to

Revelation 8:3-4. When Paul refers to the Philippians gift as both a sacrifice and a fragrant aroma, he is calling that gift *holy*, set apart, as were His people, and as we, as the "true circumcision" (v. 3:3) are, as well. God is well-pleased with their gift, Paul informs them, and will likely reward them in the same way that God rewarded obedience and sacrifice in the Jewish tradition.

Philippians 4:20-23

As Paul closes, he reminds the Philippians once more of a number of critical things. As he said, "To write the same things is no trouble to me, and it is a safeguard to you" (Philippians 3:1). He reminds them that God ought to receive all the glory, ever and always, for anything he, himself, might have accomplished in his life or in his letter to them; and likewise, He ought to receive the same glory from them in all things. He reminds them of their unity in Christ, the need to live "in harmony" (v. 4:2), to share a "same mind, maintaining the same love, united in spirit, intent on one purpose" (Philippians 2:2), and the need to see each other first as fellow worshippers of Christ, letting all else fade away in the wake of that single great truth. As Jesus said, "Truly, truly, I say to you…," so Paul sums up his entire letter in these few exhortations.

He also sends greetings from all the brethren with him in Rome. It is interesting to note that he specifically sends greeting from Caesar's household. Once again, Paul's influence, as well as that of the gospel, is evident. It was not, in fact, the Caesar, himself, Emperor Nero, who sent greetings, but those within his household who were fellow believers. Nero was one of the most powerful, most feared, most ambitious emperors of the first century. Coming to power by way of a number of political assassinations, he was known for dipping Christians in oil before lighting them on fire as entertainment in the Coliseum. He was not in any way sympathetic towards the early church, or towards Paul. No, these fellow believers to whom Paul is referring are, once again, the Praetorian Guard, whose influence was such that even at the height of his power, Nero dared not oppose them, and Paul survived, even flourished, beneath the despot emperor's nose, protected by the very men who kept him imprisoned.

What an illustration of grace Paul gives us, then, as he closes. Grace he has received from God, grace he has received from his captors, grace on Christ's behalf and grace from Christ. This grace, too, he reminds his readers of: the grace they have received, the undeserved and yet utter forgiveness of their sins from Jesus Christ. Bracketing his letter to them, Paul opened, "Grace to you and peace from God our Father and the Lord Jesus Christ" (Philippians 1:2) and closes with "The grace of the Lord Jesus Christ be with your spirit" (Philippians 4:23). Likewise, the heart of our Christian walk begins and ends in the miraculous, unspeakable grace of the Cross.

Thus does Paul close his letter to his dear friends at Philippi. With blessings, with glory to God, and with greetings from the brethren he bids them farewell. Did he ever have occasion to visit them again? We'll never know, though it is unlikely. Paul was martyred by the dreaded Nero only five years later, in 66CE. Yet, his words live on, divinely inspired. Across the centuries, Paul speaks to us as he spoke to the young Church at Philippi, his message undiminished, untarnished, as fresh and relevant today as it was two thousand years ago.

A Woven Tapestry

As we close our study of Philippians, there are several final threads that must be tucked into place and bound into the whole, completing the tapestry that Paul has woven. Within this text, we must make note of a few specific themes that were not so explicitly detailed in our study. Within the larger whole of Paul's writing, too, we must take some time to understand how the body of his work came to become the foundation and heart of our New Testament theology.

The Epistle of Joy

While there are ten different Greek words used to denote joy within the New Testament, Paul's letter to the Philippians primarily consists of only two of them: *chairō* (BLB 2016, Strong's G5463) is used 11 times to denote rejoicing, and *chara* (BLB 2016, Strong's G5479) is used 5 times to denote joy. Far from connoting mere happiness, the idea of joy goes far beyond such passing emotion, suggesting a deeper discipline of contentment in God. The author of Hebrews gives its highest example when he writes that we ought to be like Jesus, who, "for the joy [*chara*] set before Him endured the cross, despising the shame, and has sat down at the right hand of the throne of God" (Hebrews 12:2).

We have no modern context for understanding the pain and shame of crucifixion; unless one has explicitly studied the medical implications of this form of torturous death, one cannot even begin to encompass what it would have meant for the body forced to endure it. That Jesus did so, despising the shame, the pain, the mockery and derision of His captors, fixing His eyes on the joy of the Lord is, perhaps, the greatest example we can seek. As Paul said, "The things you have learned and received and heard and seen in me, practice these things, and the God of peace will be with you" (Philippians 4:9). There can be no doubt that the same would be true of Christ's example on the cross. To practice joy in the face of such overwhelming circumstances defies our comprehension, yet, to it we are called. D. Miall Edwards writes of this kind of joy, "Christian joy is no mere gaiety that knows no gloom, but is the result of the triumph of faith over adverse and trying circumstances, which, instead of hindering, actually enhance it" (Orr 1915).

What, then, do we mean when we refer to Philippians as the *Epistle of Joy*? Is it simply for its many uses of the word, or is there a deeper context? While the former is certainly true, I think the latter holds merit, as well. Barclay discusses the many joys contained within Philippians, listing them: the joy of Christian prayer (1:4), the joy that Christ is preached (1:18), the joy of faith (1:25), the joy of fellowship (2:2), the joy of suffering (2:17), the joy of hearing of a loved one (2:28), the joy of hospitality (2:29), the joy of man in Christ (3:1; 4:1), the joy of the missionary (4:1), and the joy of receiving a gift (4:10), (Barclay 1959, 16-19). While many of these certainly seem to encompass both the rejoicing of *chairō* and its celebratory attitude, we cannot overlook those joys which hint at something deeper and darker, more akin to Christ's joy on the cross. Joy in suffering might seem trite; yet remember how many times in Philippians Paul reminded his readers of their participation in the gospel, their participation in the suffering of Christ, and the glorification that, like Christ, they might hope for in the face of their persecution.

Participants in the Gospel

While joy might be one of the more prevalent themes of Philippians, unity, or Swift's *participation* is another, equally important facet of Paul's letter. Remember, again, the four ways in which Barclay illustrated the partnership of the

Philippians with the gospel, supporting Swift's premise (Barclay 1959, 21-22). The Philippians are partners in grace, partners in the work of the gospel, partners in suffering, and partners in Christ.

As partners in grace, Paul reminds the Philippians of their unity in Christ. This letter was written to the corporate whole, not simply to a single individual; and even his opening words, "grace to you and peace," remind us that it was not simply a blessing upon them, but an exhortation among them. As partners in the work of the gospel, Paul points to their participation through encouragement, through their disciplined giving, and through their faithful fellowship with one another and with him. Paul waxed eloquently on the topic of partnership in the suffering of Christ, and the Philippians' partnership with his own suffering, reminding them at every turn of the joy of the cross, set before them. He says, "that I may know Him and the power of His resurrection and the fellowship of His sufferings, being conformed to His death; in order that I might attain to the resurrection from the dead" (Philippians 3:10-11). This verse illustrates not only the former, but also the final partnership: that of being in Christ.

In fact, it seems the themes of partnership and joy, just as those of joy and suffering, become so interwoven within Paul's letter that they become symbiotic. Many of the same verses used to describe one also serve to describe the other. Remember Paul's exhortations to live "in harmony" (v. 4:2), "being of the same mind, maintaining the same love, united in spirit, and intent on one purpose" (v. 2:2). Throughout his letter, Paul echoes the theme of unity in love, unity in belief, and unity in spirit, drawing a beautiful parallel to their unity with himself – as expressed when he says, "experiencing the same conflict which you saw in me and now hear to be in me" (Philippians 1:30) – and also in Christ, which will bring the suffering of the cross, but also the glory of heaven!

Unity and Love

Finally, we must take a moment to note how many of these same themes extend across the full breadth of Paul's writings, establishing for us the foundational beliefs of our Christian understanding. The idea of our unity in Christ is further borne out by Paul's utter belief that "whether Jews of Greeks, whether slaves or free…we were all made to drink of one Spirit" (1 Corinthians 12:13). Ephesians 4 further outlines Paul's feelings on our unity in the spirit, finishing with this exhortation: "Be kind to one another, tender-hearted, forgiving each other, just as God in Christ also has forgiven you" (Ephesians 4:32). Our forgiveness from God, then, is wrapped up in our own understanding of earthly forgiveness. If God has forgiven us our greatest debts and washed us utterly clean of sin, how, then, can we do any less for our fellow believers? This is the basis, then, for the indicative statement that supports Paul's later imperative, "be subject to one another in the fear of Christ" (Ephesians 5:21). The NIV suggests this translation: "Submit to one another out of reverence for Christ." Because of who Christ is, because of what He has done for us, we, then, ought to do the same to our fellow man, with whom we have so much more commonality in our shared sinful nature. As my son prays nightly, "Forgive us our debts, as we forgive our debtors" (Matthew 6:12, NIV).

On a more uplifting note, Paul returns to this theme of unity, again, in Colossians, when he says, "that their hearts may be encouraged, having been knit together in love, and attaining to all the wealth that comes from the full assurance of understanding, resulting in a true knowledge of God's mystery, that is, Christ Himself" (Colossians 2:2). While a complex statement, the implication is that in being united in love, we are assured a full understanding of the great mystery of God. If His love for us and for His son was enough to cover over all of our sins, how much more will the mystery of Christ be revealed to us when we allow our love for others to form the foundational principle of our hearts and minds. Paul later goes on to sum this up by saying, "Beyond all these things put on love, which is the perfect bond of unity" (Colossians 3:14).

In Ephesians, Paul returns to these twin themes, writing, "Therefore I, the prisoner of the Lord, implore you to walk in a manner worthy of the calling with which you have been called, with all humility and gentleness, with patience, showing tolerance for one another in love, being diligent to preserve the unity of the Spirit in the bond of peace" (Ephesians 4:1-3). The following verses go on to outline our one-ness, or unity, in Christ and in each other (the body). If I didn't know better, I might think I was back in Philippians again! Paul's reminder that we ought to live as Citizens of Heaven (see also Ephesians 5:15-16), that we ought to be patient with one another, living in harmony because of our faith seem plucked from those verses, yet this letter is to a completely different church. Though written around the same time as Philippians, Ephesians was a much more forceful letter, responding to a number of challenges the church at Ephesus was facing, but it, too, steeps itself in Paul's central tenets.

It is interesting to note that Christ, Himself, said the greatest commandment was to "love the Lord your God with all your heart, and with all your soul, and with all your mind," then continued, "You shall love your neighbor as yourself" (Matthew 22:37, 39). Jesus summed up the entire Old

Testament teaching with these two commands. It is no wonder, then, that love became a central theme of every New Testament writer as they wrestled with this emerging new theology of grace, mercy, and love as the pillars of a previously rule-bound religion. Gone was the judgement of the Law, replaced, now, by this somewhat nebulous new philosophy. Paul says,

> If I speak with the tongues of men and of angels, but do not have love, I have become a noisy gong or a clanging cymbal. If I have the gift of prophecy, and know all mysteries and all knowledge; and if I have all faith, so as to remove mountains, but do not have love, I am nothing. And if I give all my possessions to feed the poor, and if I surrender my body to be burned, but do not have love, it profits me nothing. (1 Corinthians 13:1-3)

He ends these verses with two declarations: "love never fails" (1 Corinthians 13:8) and "the greatest of these is love" (1 Corinthians 13:13). As Paul counted all his earthly riches, possessions, titles, and glory rubbish before God, so, too, are every gift and skill we might possess without it being united in this great command to love.

Love God and love others; that is enough. In loving God, it is impossible not to love others; and in loving others, we show the same grace and mercy we, ourselves, have received, closing the circle of faith and works.

The Journey's End

Ten years after he first visited the city of Philippi in Macedonia, Paul wrote to their fellowship a letter that echoes across the centuries. As we have now followed Paul's journey from Acts to Philippians, and beyond, as well, I can't help but be reminded of where we started: a sharp disagreement, a paroxysm between two men that threatened to rend the early church, a fiery Paul, unwilling to bend, and a friendship in ruins.

In Philippians 3, Paul speaks of his lineage as he prepares to describe all that he has cast aside for the glory of Christ. He says, "circumcised the eighth day, of the nation of Israel, of the tribe of Benjamin, a Hebrew of Hebrews" (Philippians 3:5). When Jacob prophesied over his many sons at the close of Genesis, he said this of his youngest son: "Benjamin is a ravenous wolf; in the morning he devours the prey, and in the evening he divides the spoil" (Genesis 49:27).

Throughout the Old Testament, the rash, war-like nature of the Tribe of Benjamin fulfills this prophecy. Paul seems a worthy heir to this tradition, both as Saul – where he was, indeed, like a ravenous wolf, devouring followers of Christ – and later, as a young Christian, with his impassioned, sometimes intemperate temper. It would be hard to miss the many ways in which his later testimony to the churches of the New Testament stand in stark contrast to his own actions in Acts.

Somewhere along the way, Paul changed. He laid aside the bloodline that had brought him so much pride, set his crowns at Christ's feet, and received the grace and mercy that God has promised. While it might be easy to believe this could happen in an instant, the reality is that few deliveries from God are so stark. It is in the journey, after all, that we learn the truth of God's intimate presence, that we practice love, contentment, faith, and joy. While the destination is a worthy goal, it is the journey that lends our hearts to mercy and compassion for those who follow after us.

It is Paul's journey, then, that lends him the credibility and credence to lead the early European churches. In the same way, it is the journey of those who walked beside him that pave the trails for our own steps. Paul spent only a few days in Philippi, yet those precious brethren shaped his ministry for over a decade. Their faithful gifts supported

Paul's work again and again, their prayers protected him, their dear friendship fortified him.

At a small, rural prosthetics clinic in Kenya, one of our team, a Biology major, felt God's call: to become a missionary Ob/Gyn in Africa. In the off hand, yet completely genuine manner of the young at heart, we promised that when the time came, we would support her work. Eight years later, she had graduated from medical school and had finished her residency. We received a postcard from Samaritan's Purse, "Dear Friends, I'm asking for your support…" She is now in her first year at a medical clinic in the Democratic Republic of Congo and has experienced both tremendous success and devastating failure. Her second child was recently born in the very clinic in which she works. We have been blessed to participate with her in the gospel of Christ, to suffer with her when she grieves over a mother or child not saved, to rejoice in the many perfect infants born into her hands, to walk beside her in her calling in Christ. Yet, it all began with two words: *Dear Friends…*

Finally, beloved, as we close, if I have any hope, it is this: I hope the printed words of your Bible have leapt off the page, captured your attention, and exploded into living color. I hope that you have found in this study something rousing and relevant. So easily our study time can devolve into boredom and tedium, eyes skittering over empty words scattered across a page without every really seeing them. Having studied Paul, his travels, his life, and his writing, the lens through which I read his letters has been drastically changed. While they are written in a communal sense, they seem more intimate these days, more personal, like a beloved confidante penning words from their heart directly to my eyes, and ears, and spirit. I hope, and believe in faith, the same for you.

Like Paul, the temper of my own youth seems to slowly be giving way to the work of God in me. I am certainly not perfect, yet his words seem to echo in my own mind, "for it is God who is at work in you" (Philippians 2:13). I am not perfect, yet I press on. I am imperfect, yet being perfected in Christ. So, too, are you, dear friend, beloved. So, go forth and journey on. How could I say it better than Paul? "The grace of the Lord Jesus Christ be with your spirit." Amen.

Bibliography

2016. *BLB*. Accessed December 15, 2015. https://www.blueletterbible.org/.

Andrews, Evan. 2014. *8 Things You May Not Know About the Praetorian Guard – History Lists*. July 8. Accessed October 15, 2015. http://www.history.com/news/history-lists/8-things-you-may-not-know-about-the-praetorian-guard.

Barclay, William. 1959. *The Letters to the Philippians, Colossians, and Thessalonians*. Philadelphia, PA: Westminster Press.

Barker, Kenneth L., ed. 2014. "Intro to Philippians – Biblica." *Biblica*. January 15. Accessed August 11, 2015. http://www.biblica.com/en-us/bible/online-bible/scholar-notes/niv-study-bible/intro-to-philippians/.

Bruce, F. F. 1988. *The Book of Acts*. Grand Rapids, MI: Wm. B. Eerdmans Publishing Co.

CK. 2015. "The Focus of our Faith." Snohomish, WA, April.

Cottrell, T. 2009."Beth Moore Feature." *Jesus Saves (Live)*. 10.

Easton, Matthew. 1897a. "Fear of the Lord the – Easton's Bible Dictionary." *StudyLight*. Accessed November 7, 2015. https://www.studylight.org/dictionaries/ebd/view.cgi?n=1317.
—. 1897b. "Jailer – Easton's Bible Dictionary." *StudyLight*. Accessed March 11, 2016. http://www.studylight.org/dictionaries/ebd/view.cgi?n=1958.

File, Thom. 2013. "The Diversifying Electorate—Voting Rates by Race and Hispanic Origin in 2012 (and Other Recent Elections)." *United States Census Bureau*. May. Accessed November 2, 2015. http://www.census.gov/prod/2013pubs/p20-568.pdf.

Gibbon, Edward. 1776. *The History of the Decline and Fall of the Roman Empire*. Vol. 1. 6 vols. London.

Gill, John. 1999. "Acts 16 Commentary – John Gill's Exposition of the Entire Bible." *StudyLight*. Accessed July 6, 2015. https://www.studylight.org/commentaries/geb/acts-16.html.

Guzik, David. 2001a. "Study Guide for Acts 9 by David Guzik." *Blue Letter Bible*. Accessed June 24, 2015. https://www.blueletterbible.org/Comm/guzik_david/StudyGuide_Act/Act_9.cfm?a=1027001.

—. 2001b. "Study Guide for Acts 13 by David Guzik." *Blue Letter Bible*. Accessed June 24, 2015. https://www.blueletterbible.org/Comm/guzik_david/StudyGuide_Act/Act_13.cfm?a=1031001.

—. 2001c. "Study Guide for Acts 16 by David Guzik." *Blue Letter Bible*. Accessed August 3, 2015. https://www.blueletterbible.org/Comm/guzik_david/StudyGuide_Act/Act_16.cfm?a=1034001.

—. 2006a. "Study Guide for Philippians 1 by David Guzik." *Blue Letter Bible*. Accessed October 26, 2015. https://www.blueletterbible.org/Comm/guzik_david/StudyGuide_Phl/Phl_1.cfm?a=1104001.

—. 2006b. "Study Guide for Philippians 2 by David Guzik." *Blue Letter Bible*. Accessed November 4, 2015. https://www.blueletterbible.org/Comm/guzik_david/StudyGuide_Phl/Phl_2.cfm.

—. 2006c. "Study Guide for Philippians 3 by David Guzik." *Blue Letter Bible.* Accessed November 23, 2015. https://www.blueletterbible.org/Comm/guzik_david/Study Guide_Phl/Phl_3.cfm?a=1106001.

—. 2006d. "Study Guide for Philippians 4 by David Guzik." *Blue Letter Bible.* Accessed January 20, 2016. https://www.blueletterbible.org/Comm/guzik_david/Study Guide_Phl/Phl_4.cfm?a=1107001.

Hall, Katie. 2016. "Letters to the Church: Philippians." *BibleGateway.* Accessed November 2, 2015. http://www.biblegateway.com/blog/2012/08/letters-to-the-church-philippians/.

Help :: Help Tutorials. n.d. Accessed April 5, 2016. https://www.blueletterbible.org/help/BLBStrongs.cfm.

Henry, Matthew. 1706a. "Philippians 2 Commentary – Matthew Henry's Concise Commentary on the Bible." *StudyLight.* Accessed November 23, 2015. https://www.studylight.org/commentaries/mhn/philippians-2.html.

—. 1706b. "Philippians Overview – Matthew Henry's Concise Commentary on the Bible." *StudyLight*. Accessed August 15, 2015. https://www.studylight.org/commentaries/mhn/philippians-0.html.

Herrick, Greg. 2004. *Introduction, Background, and Outline to Philippians*. June 29. Accessed September 15, 2015. https://bible.org/seriespage/introduction-background-and-outline-philippians#P92_10758.

Jahnige, Joan. 2002. *KET DL | Latin 1 | Mores | Roman Law and Government*. May. Accessed November 10, 2015. http://www.dl.ket.org/latin1/mores/law/citizenship.htm.

Jamieson, Robert, A. R. Fausset, and David Brown. 1882. "Commentary on Philippians 2 by Jamieson, Fausset & Brown." *Blue Letter Bible*. Accessed November 6, 2015. https://www.blueletterbible.org/Comm/jfb/Phl/Phl_002.cfm.

Johnson, Allan Chester, Paul Robinson Coleman-Norton, and Frank Card Bourne. 1961. *The Avalon Project: The Twelve Tables*. Edited by Clyde Pharr. University of Texas Press, Austin. Accessed November 2, 2015. http://avalon.law.yale.edu/ancient/twelve_tables.asp.

Lapin, Danial. 2010. *Thou Shall Prosper: Ten Commandments for Making Money*. Hoboken, NJ: John Wiley & Sons Inc.

Meyer, F. B. n.d. "Philippians 3 Commentary – F.B. Meyer's Devotional Commentary." *StudyLight*. Accessed November 23, 2015. http://www.studylight.org/commentaries/dcp/philippians-3.html#bibliography.

Moore, Beth. 2011. *Mercy Triumphs*. Nashville, TN: LifeWay Press.

—. 2014. *Children of the Day*. Nashville, TN: LifeWay Press.

Orr, James. 1915. "Joy – International Standard Bible Encyclodepia." *StudyLight*. Accessed February 1, 2016. https://www.studylight.org/encyclopedias/isb/view.cgi?n=5124.

Shirer, Patricia. 2015. "The Armor of God." *The Armor of God.* Nashville: LifeWay Christian Resources.

Smallwood, E. Mary. 2001. *The Jews Under Roman Rule: From Pompey to Diocletian: A Study in Political Relations.* Brill Academic Publishers.

Smith, William. 1901. "Minister – Smith's Bible Dictionary." *StudyLight.* Accessed November 17, 2015. https://www.studylight.org/dictionaries/sbd/view.cgi?n=30 07.

Spurgeon, Charles H. 1893. "Spurgeon's Sermons Volume 39: 1893." *Christian Classics Ethereal Library.* Accessed November 23, 2015.
http://www.ccel.org/ccel/spurgeon/sermons39.xxvii.html.
—. 1895. "Spurgeon's Sermons Volume 41: 1895." *Christian Classics Ethereal Library.* Accessed January 20, 2016. http://www.ccel.org/ccel/spurgeon/sermons41.xii.html.
—. 1910. "Spurgeon on Philippians." *PreceptAustin.* August 4. Accessed January 11, 2016.
http://www.preceptaustin.org/spurgeon_on_philippians1.ht m.

Swift, Robert. 1984. "Swift: The Theme and Structure of Philippians." Accessed August 15, 2015. https://faculty.gordon.edu/hu/bi/ted_hildebrandt/ntesources/ntarticles/bsac-nt/swift-philipstruct-bs.htm.

Vines, W. E. 1940a. "Affection, Affected – Vine's Expository Dictionary of NT Words." *StudyLight*. Accessed October 19, 2015. https://www.studylight.org/dictionaries/ved/view.cgi?n=56.

—. 1940b. "Hazard – Vine's Expository Dictionary of NT Words." *StudyLight*. Accessed November 17, 2015. https://www.studylight.org/dictionaries/ved/view.cgi?n=1321.

Walker, W. L. 1939. "Fear – International Standard Bible Encyclopedia." *International Standard Bible Encyclopedia Online*. Edited by James Orr. Accessed November 7, 2015. http://www.internationalstandardbible.com/F/fear.html.

Wuest, Kenneth. 2015. *Philippians 3:7-8 Commentary*. November 30. Accessed January 11, 2016. http://www.preceptaustin.org/philippians_37-11.htm.

www.openbible.info. 2012. *Calculating the Time and Cost of Paul's Missionary Journeys*. July 5. Accessed July 21, 2015. http://www.openbible.info/blog/2012/07/calculating-the-time-and-cost-of-pauls-missionary-journeys/.

Yancey, Phillip. 1995. *The Jesus I Never Knew*. Grand Rapids, MI: Zondervan.

Zondervan. 2014. "NIV Study Bible." *Biblica*. Edited by Kenneth L. Barker. January 15. Accessed August 11, 2015. http://www.biblica.com/en-us/bible/online-bible/scholar-notes/niv-study-bible/intro-to-philippians/.

About the Author

Rebecca Minelga is a graduate of LeTourneau University in Longview, Texas, where she studied liberal arts with an emphasis on the impact of Christian culture on history and literature. She is an author and speaker who uses the power of words to navigate the liminal spaces between who we are and who we are becoming. She raises Guide Dog Puppies and two sons - in that order - with her husband just north of Seattle. She has been previously published in *The Mark Literary Review*, *Crêpe and Penn*, and *The Hooghly Review*. Discover more about her at rminelga.wordpress.com.

www.ingramcontent.com/pod-product-compliance
Lightning Source LLC
Chambersburg PA
CBHW070542010526
44118CB00012B/1196